WOMEN NOW

WOMEN NOW

THE LEGACY OF FEMALE SUFFRAGE

**EDITOR
BRONWYN
LABRUM**

TE PAPA
PRESS

CONTENTS

INTRODUCTION / 7
Bronwyn Labrum

THE POWER OF THE WORD / 21
Barbara Brookes

LIVES ON THE LINE / 37
Sue Bradford

OUR COUNTRY'S MIRROR / 51
Morgan Godfery

UNFINISHED BUSINESS / 65
Sandra Coney

PLAYING WITH FIRE / 81
Fiona Kidman

WHAT WILL I TELL MY DAUGHTERS? / 95
Holly Walker

AT THE FOREFRONT / 109
Ben Schrader

LET'S FIX THIS / 125
Golriz Ghahraman

MRS SHEPPARD AND MR SEDDON / 139
Megan Whelan

PAO PAO PAO / 155
Tina Makereti

A RADICAL NOTION / 169
Charlotte Macdonald

FEMINIST ENOUGH? / 183
Grace Taylor

ABOUT THE CONTRIBUTORS / 199

FURTHER READING / 205

ACKNOWLEDGEMENTS / 207

**BRONWYN
LABRUM**

INTRODUCTION

Posters, badges and tea towels with galvanising phrases; pamphlets, medals, banknotes, works of art, contraceptive pills . . . Objects tell the history of women's rights in a myriad of ways from the everyday to the extraordinary. Increasingly museums are collecting the objects of activism and protest, of people's lives and causes, often from ordinary members of the public and from mass movements. In 2017, the online Merriam-Webster dictionary judged 'feminism' as its word of the year: it was 'a top lookup throughout the year, with several spikes that corresponded to various news reports and events'.[1] The dictionary defines feminism as 'the theory of the political, economic, and social equality of the sexes' and 'organized activity on behalf of women's rights and interests'.[2]

After the global women's marches, the release of Margaret Atwood's dystopian novel *The Handmaid's Tale* as a television series, the #MeToo movement of openness about sexual assault in various industries and institutions, wearing black or carrying white roses on the red carpet, and a more general unease about the relations between the sexes in the twenty-first century, this groundswell of attention was not surprising. Many women were wondering how far equality between the sexes had actually been realised and why feminism seems still to be so necessary.

They wanted to know what more could be done. The international movements all had their direct impact on Aotearoa New Zealand, as this renewed interest was globalised and interconnected. This upsurge in talking, thinking and organising coincided with the national celebration in New Zealand of the one hundred and twenty-fifth anniversary of women's suffrage and provided the impetus for the publication of this book.

This is the first volume in Te Papa Press's 'Thinking About . . .' series, which links to the museum's aspiration to be a 'safe place for difficult conversations'. This inaugural title brings together provocative, insightful and energetically argued essays by 12 leading New Zealand writers and thinkers on the situation of New Zealand women since 1893 and the challenges ahead. It is designed to stimulate debate and ongoing conversations. Each writer was given an object of significance to the history of New Zealand women from Te Papa's collection and asked to respond to the object in whichever way they chose. As each essay appeared in my inbox, I realised even more clearly the importance of these conversations, this thinking and writing, this book.

As Sue Bradford notes, we live in 'dangerous times'. All of the authors exhort us to action and, as Sandra Coney concludes, 'There is a big job ahead of us, but 2018 seems a very good year to start the mahi.' I thank the authors for responding enthusiastically and expressively to the challenge I gave them and for providing such powerful personal observations.

As I worked on this book, it became ever more evident how important a national museum collection is to the task of reflection, conversation and action. When I wrote *Women's History: A short guide to researching and writing women's history* for the centenary of women's suffrage in 1993, I still had to make the case for focusing on women in history and then to suggest how this might be done. I showed how many topics in women's history were still to be investigated, and I pointed out how much we had to learn. In 2018, by contrast, it is relatively easy to assemble a range of objects from 1893 to the present to materialise aspects of women's rights and women's issues, although of course there are still huge gaps in our knowledge and understanding. The objects in this book focus on public campaigns, cultural forms and institutions, and conventional forms of advocacy (even if the content was never conventional).

As part of its Suffrage 125 programme,[3] Te Papa's curators are on a drive to collect more objects that broaden and deepen our understanding and provide us with more access to everyday and hidden histories of a wider range of women. There are also clear gaps over time: we know far more about the public campaigns of the 1890s and 1970s onwards, but we need to do more research on the 1920s and '30s and the immediate postwar period. I hope that you may be inspired to compile your own list of objects, and help your local museum collect them.

In these pages you will read about important individuals, such as Kate Sheppard, the leader of the suffrage campaign in New Zealand, who towers over the history of women's rights. Barbara Brookes writes about a Women's Christian Temperance Union pamphlet and that organisation's publication strategy and desires in the wake of gaining the vote. Suffrage was a beginning, not an end, and WCTU members desired above all to make New Zealand a better place for women and children, based on the 'moral uplifting of humanity'. Global connections and currents were as evident in 1893, when women in New Zealand were finally able to vote, as they are in the present. As Charlotte Macdonald observes, in 2018 Kate Sheppard is in our pockets, our purses, our wallets and handbags. Exploring her portrait on the $10 banknote, she suggests that we probably do not think much about her or her contemporaries' long campaign for women's economic independence from men. Macdonald challenges us while using this note in everyday transactions to ponder: What kind of fairness has the world made for us?

Sue Bradford explores the experiences of Frances Parker, a New Zealand-born suffragette in Scotland who was awarded a medal for valour on hunger strikes by the Women's Social and Political Union in 1912. Her story is one we can add to the pantheon of individual heroines. As well as reminding us of how long it took British women to be enfranchised, the account of Parker's militant actions and imprisonments, and the medal bestowed, underlines a less familiar mode of operating, albeit one brought to wider notice with the 2015 film *Suffragette*. Deftly weaving between Parker's and her own history of direct action, Bradford argues that 'our solidarity from collective militant action can be a powerful force. Ordinary people, acting together, can make change.' The 'exquisite madness' of Parker can and should be parlayed into 'emancipatory organising and action'.

Other objects celebrate battles seemingly won. Sandra Coney explores the stamp that commemorated the seventy-fifth anniversary of universal suffrage in 1968, the year that was

INTRODUCTION

declared the International Year for Human Rights. A 'curious' stamp 'redolent of order and calm', it belied the fact that so much remained to be achieved — and, furthermore, that trouble lay on the horizon. As Coney recounts, over the 75 years between the vote and the celebratory stamp, women continued to fight: for the right to stand for Parliament, to serve on juries and to work while married, as well as for reproductive rights and equal pay among other goals. She also notes that the fight for women's rights 'was not seen as part of a wider struggle by indigenous peoples, Afro-Americans, workers, youth and so on'. There would be no agreed-upon, finally arrived at status quo that meant women everywhere had achieved equality.

This fact is underlined by Golriz Ghahraman's consideration of equal pay campaigns. Contemplating the Clerical Workers Union tea towel and the witty cartoon of a boy and girl comparing the difference in their genitalia, she wryly observes, 'What cannot be expressed via tea-towel art is likely not worth contemplating.' Arguing against rising apathy and the pressure that the assumption of equality places on women, she alerts us to even more pressure on women and girls: 'we attempt to meet impossible standards on all fronts — from career, to home, to our very feminine forms — while being told we are more or less "post gender"'. Ghahraman's cogently argued essay shows how one object — a tea towel — 'crystallises . . . not only the unfairness of the gender pay gap, but also the fact that women today have the difficult task of proving gender discrimination still exists at all, despite achievement of formal equality and decades of persistent activism'. Her plea to listen to women and to affirm varied experiences of unfairness is one that we should heed.

Mass campaigns and marches, such as those for equal pay, are the quintessential public face of feminism. Another group of objects in this collection will be very familiar to women of a certain generation, often called 'second-wave' feminists (after the first 'great wave' in the nineteenth century). By the mid-1970s, the women's movement had succeeded in making 'women's liberation' a household term and the United Nations General Assembly proclaimed 1975 International Women's Year.

The New Zealand government duly established the Committee on Women, which proclaimed that 'women can do anything'. Among their posters is one that shows women at work as nurses, taxi drivers, gardeners, machine operators, truck drivers, butchers, judges and road workers. The logo for the Committee on Women comprised a dove and a female symbol. Holly Walker, who stepped down from being an MP before the 2014 election, cautions us: '"Having it all". That old chestnut. The evil cousin of "Women can do anything"; now we must do everything.' Despite the optimism of the campaign badge she writes about, Walker recounts her anguish at not being able to combine work as an MP and motherhood. She asks: 'I grew up believing women can do anything. What will I tell my daughters?'

I invited two men to write for this collection, in the belief that equality should be a shared goal. Ben Schrader took on the challenge of writing about the 'Women against the Tour' badge from the infamous winter of discontent in 1981, when the Springboks were touring New Zealand against the All Blacks. As he notes, many people wore jackets or coats 'swathed in badges of all colours and sizes', and although he doesn't remember this particular one he does recall clearly that 'women and girls were at the forefront of attempts to stop the tour'. Schrader's acute recollections form a mental picture of the many women involved:

> I see my schoolmate Sarah, vigorously discussing ideas and tactics in the library, dressed in her punk T-shirt and overcoat. I see [my sister] Kay's distressed face following the Battle of Molesworth Street. I also see a montage of the women who were fleetingly beside me on protests; their hats and scarves tightly secured against the bitterness.

He argues strongly that the Springbok tour languishes in our collective memory of that decade, coming low in the order of significance after the 1984 snap election, Rogernomics (neoliberalism), the nuclear-free policy, and the stock market crash of 1987. His essay is a plea to recall the women the badge represents and 'to remember more deeply and more critically' the series of events that divided a nation, communities and families.

A group of essays discuss art and artworks — a useful reminder that feminism and equality had a cultural dimension beyond politics, economics and the material life. Morgan

Godfery meditates on Margaret Butler's sculpture *La Nouvelle Zélande,* modelled on the Māori dancer Miriama Heketa. 'At every moment in this country's history . . . women are at the very centre of social life. And yet they are rarely at the centre of politics or art.' Rather than see Butler's sculpture as a conservative or conventional work of art, Godfery argues that its genius lies in returning Māori women to the centre of New Zealand life; indeed, they *are* New Zealand. What, he asks, might it mean to look at our country from the perspective of Māori women and the crueller social, economic and cultural spaces they currently occupy?

Tina Makereti unpacks her own story about an 'art object and artefact, political statement and taonga' that is 'first of all a poi'. Describing and retelling a story of power and grace, Makereti ruminates on her origins and upbringing, noting that although she, too, is from Parihaka, like the maker of the poi, she didn't grow up there and her family left the region in waves from the nineteenth century. Of mixed blood, Makereti was, in her words, born of Māori soil and grew out of goddesses, all of which gives her an understanding of women's power and roles. She notes that 'women run families and nations and always have. Men work alongside them in these tasks because they always have. At the centre, the children.' Indeed, as she puts it, '"Man" given rights mean little when you know you are descended from the goddesses of life and death.' For Makereti, this poi was personally transforming and is an intensely personal example of how 'art can connect and transform and bring you back in touch with that which you think you have lost'.

Access to art and to women's art in public spaces is not something that can be taken for granted. Using the Guerrilla Girls' public cultural campaigns as her starting point, Megan Whelan takes us on a peripatetic personal and political tour through tea towels, tattoos and memorials. She wonders why we are so bad at commemorating women and asks why, given the early enfranchising of women, 'are we so coy about women's successes?' Pointing out the Guerrilla Girls' insistent use of fact and humour to expose gender and ethnic bias in politics, art, film and popular culture, Whelan reminds herself that in her public role as a radio broadcaster she must remember to 'keep on being the harpy', just as the first and subsequent generations of feminists were.

Our insistent demands for the vote, equality and visibility are arguments for freedom: freedom to be, to do, to achieve, to participate fully in society and public life. The final two essays speak directly to this aspect. Fiona Kidman offers an intimate perspective on the contraceptive pill, available in New Zealand from 1961. Before then, Kidman describes how women lived:

> Terror, that's what it was. We lived in terror. Our bodies were ready for sex whether or not we had yet to find the right mate but, back then, in the 1950s, the results could deliver shame and grief in equal measure, possible rejection by our parents, the lonely desperate giving of birth in cruel and unfeeling surroundings, the loss of children, bitterness and shame.

But although the Pill seemed like a miracle, it was not a panacea. Making a clarion call for abortion to be legal and accessible, Kidman concludes her essay with the hope that controlling fertility will be seen as not just a personal freedom, but also as 'a measure of social justice and equality, and of improved relationships between the sexes'.

In early 2017, after the inauguration of President Trump in the United States, women around the globe marched against his infamous remarks about women's genitalia and out of a fear that women's rights were at risk. The pussy hat became the indelible symbol of this upwelling of activism. Under the critical gaze of Grace Taylor, however, the pussy hat represents a step back in history: essentialist and demeaning. Puzzling about this leads her to a poetic exploration of feminism and freedom animated by fear that, in our era of social media, we are egged on to exhibit a 'strange, slightly contrived sense of displaying your goddess'. Not a feminist herself, Taylor asks: 'How can I honour and empower myself as a woman and mother in ways that also empower others?' She argues that 'feminism = freedom. Freedom to evolve, to adapt when required, to respond with urgency and love.' Taylor's essay usefully reminds us that there is diversity and disagreement as well as common ground between women now, as in the past, and that there is no one set of answers to the questions raised by feminist activism.

INTRODUCTION

In thinking about women now, at the beginning of the twenty-first century, it is clear that there is a long way still to go. The remarkable intellectual ability, organising prowess and international connectedness of the suffrage campaign in the 1890s, represented here by a pamphlet and a banknote, is a legacy that should make us think, join in the conversations, and act. The diverse objects and writers assembled in this book make this abundantly clear. There are unresolved issues, rights still to be gained or to be gained more equitably, and many other challenges to overcome, such as those from individuals and groups who are not white and middle-class. Moreover, the super-diversity of New Zealand and the unacceptable divergence in wealth we are currently witnessing, as well as the untapped potential of Māori and Pasifika, should make us redouble our efforts. What will *you* do to advance women's rights and equality in 2018 and beyond?

1   Merriam-Webster.com, https://www.merriam-webster.com/words-at-play/word-of-the-year-2017-feminism.

2   Merriam-Webster.com, https://www.merriam-webster.com/dictionary/feminism.

3   Suffrage 125 is a government-sponsored Tier 1 Commemoration that marks the one hundred and twenty-fifth anniversary of women's suffrage in New Zealand. It is led by the Ministry for Women and supported by the Ministry for Culture and Heritage. https://mch.govt.nz/suffrage-125.

**BARBARA
BROOKES**

THE
POWER
OF THE
WORD

FRANCHISE REPORT

FOR 1893

OF THE NEW ZEALAND

WOMEN'S CHRISTIAN TEMPERANCE UNION.

This Circular can be transmitted by post for a half-penny.

WARD, WILSON, AND CO, PRINTERS, INVERCARGILL, N.Z.

TITLE:	Franchise Report for 1893 of The New Zealand Women's Christian Temperance Union
PRODUCTION:	New Zealand Women's Christian Temperance Union, 1893 Ward / Wilson and Co.
MATERIALS:	Paper, printing ink
DIMENSIONS:	222 (width) x 289 (height) mm
REGISTRATION:	CA000383/001/0026

A simple pamphlet, a key way of communicating with adherents to a nineteenth-century national cause, raises a myriad of questions. Why was this pamphlet, written by Christchurch-based Kate Sheppard, printed in Invercargill? Did Sheppard telegraph or mail her copy to her southern printer? Did every printing house look kindly on women's suffrage or were particular printers known to be well disposed to the women's cause? Who designed it, with its six different fonts on the front and the elegant border? How many copies were printed and how many read? The survival of such fragile pamphlets — known in the library world as ephemera — prompts the reader to explore new avenues of historical research. If I had seen this in a second-hand bookshop, I would have scooped it up.

There is something about holding documents produced at the time I am researching that moves me — be they pamphlets, court records, casebooks or letters. It was that sense of being in touch with the past that led me to become a historian. I do have my own piece of suffrage ephemera, so precious to me that I had it specially framed to present both sides. I chose purple, green and white surrounds for the front image, since they were the suffrage colours. This piece of paper — a throwaway printed-card programme — is on the wall of my study and I often contemplated it while working on my *History of New Zealand Women*.

Given to me when I was a graduate student living in England in 1981, studying the then disreputable topic of backstreet abortion, the programme was issued for the public meeting to commemorate the enfranchisement of women, held at the city hall in Cardiff, Wales, on 5 July 1918. My landlady (I lived in a bedsit in her house) was the daughter of an English suffragist and had become a doctor, since her mother believed that women should take up a profession. It was an unhappy choice for her — living out the dreams of her activist mother — but she loved my interest in women's history, told me all sorts of fascinating things about her past, and found me people to talk to about their experiences of abortion. She gave me her mother's carefully preserved programme. On one side is an illustration of a Joan of Arc-type figure holding a flag entitled 'Woman's Franchise'. Underneath the image are the words 'AT LAST!' and overwritten there is the signature, in pencil, of the leader of the constitutional suffragists, Millicent Garrett Fawcett. I treasure this gift from Silvia Mehta.

No doubt the New Zealand Women's Christian Temperance Union issued many programmes of celebratory meetings when the suffrage was won, but I've never seen one. People often don't keep such things and when they do, their descendants, for whom they are often meaningless, are quick to get rid of them. Fortunately a number of WCTU pamphlets survive, reprinting talks of note or advice they thought others might find useful. Their pamphlet on 'Economic Cooking Lessons', for example, reached its third edition by 1889. In her 'Hints to District Franchise Superintendents', published in the WCTU page of *The Prohibitionist* in February 1892, Kate Sheppard advised, 'Keep as good a stock of franchise literature on hand as funds will allow; books to lend, if feasible, but certainly pamphlets, leaflets, etc.'[1] Pamphlets were freely distributed at places where people gathered, such as agricultural shows. Sheppard keenly followed events abroad and collected literature by overseas suffrage societies, reminding her readers they were part of an international movement. Educating the public about women's suffrage was an urgent matter, and she believed in the power of the word to change minds.

There were many matters to be set to rights in the late 1890s: first and foremost, the drinking problem. Women witnessed the devastating impact of alcohol within their communities. Trouble brewed in public houses, where men might take their daily wages and could easily drink the money away, going home empty-handed. If women objected, violence might erupt. The number and rowdiness of public houses made the streets unsafe and accidents common. The rapid growth of the WCTU in New Zealand after the visit of Mary Leavitt, an American WCTU missionary who toured the world campaigning against alcohol in 1885, attests to the strength of feeling against the drink trade amongst middle-class women.

High rates of drunkenness were common in colonial societies, giving impetus to the fight against alcohol. But the American founder of WCTU, Frances Willard, urged women to 'do everything' since she believed all social problems to be interconnected. Kate Sheppard quickly recognised this when she assisted with a petition to Parliament arguing against the employment of barmaids. When it was ignored, she realised that women had to have the vote to effect change. As the head of the WCTU Franchise and Legislation Section from 1887,

Sheppard developed a publication strategy to educate the public.

She began at the top. In May 1888 all members of the House of Representatives received a WCTU leaflet entitled 'Ten Reasons Why the Women of New Zealand Should Vote'. The first read: 'Because a democratic government like that of New Zealand already admits the great principle that every adult person, not convicted of crime, nor suspected of lunacy, has an inherent right to vote in the construction of laws which all must obey.'[2] Sheppard was keenly aware of the arguments made by opponents of the women's cause, which she listed in another leaflet: that 'the franchise would make woman unwomanly', that 'she would neglect her home duties on account of it', that 'it would cause dissension between husband and wife', that 'giving women the franchise would only be giving dual votes to married men', that 'because she cannot fight she should not vote', that 'because of motherhood she has no time to vote', that 'it would demoralise women to associate with men at the polling-booths', that 'women are already represented by their fathers, brothers or sons', and that 'women do not want to vote'.[3] One by one she rebutted these arguments and encouraged others to do so both in print and on public platforms.

The 1893 Franchise Report was produced at a time of jubilation that women's suffrage had been won. Marian Hatton sent a telegram reporting the Dunedin celebration on 20 September: 'Splendid meeting last night. City Hall crammed mostly women. Enthusiasm unbounded. Thousand handkerchiefs waving for victory.'[4] In the report, Sheppard allowed herself only to express modest 'gratification'. Yet this was an account of an international first: a nation recognising the right of adult women to vote. Sheppard insisted that it was the 'unceasing energy' of WCTU members, who had brought this victory about by means of petitions, which played a vital educational role. The willing volunteers were the ones who overcame the disadvantage of New Zealand's geography, with its widely scattered population, and succeeded in obtaining over 31,000 signatures to support women's suffrage.

This point was quickly forgotten. William Lovell-Smith felt moved to publish his *Outlines of the Women's Franchise Movement in New Zealand* in 1905 after reading William Pember Reeves' *State Experiments in Australia and New Zealand* (1902), in which Reeves wrote: 'So one fine morning of September 1893, the women of New Zealand woke up and found themselves enfranchised. The privilege was theirs, given freely and spontaneously in the easiest and most unexpected manner in the world by male politicians . . . No franchise leagues had fought the fight year after year . . .'[5]

In eliding the work of women, Reeves joined a long historical tradition. The generation of historians of women that shaped me from the 1970s onwards worked to overturn that tradition.

What kind of world did Kate Sheppard imagine would result from the path-breaking reform of women's suffrage? The pamphlet suggests that the greatest hope of the WCTU was that it would lead to the 'moral uplifting of humanity'. Sheppard and the women's movement of the nineteenth century were acutely aware of the 'humiliating fact' that there was 'one law for a man and another for a woman'.[6] Up until 1892, the electoral law excluded women from the definition of 'person'. Sheppard noted that as a woman was 'not a person, she must necessarily have been a "thing"' and that '"things" are possessed and owned'. This suited a number of men who regarded women as created solely for their pleasure and not capable of independent thought and action.[7] In fact men who opposed women's suffrage objected to 'strong-minded women', to which Sheppard replied that for 'some men, in A.D. 1892, the ideal woman is feeble-minded!'[8]

A morally principled nation, committed to justice and equity, would see women as full participants in social and political life. Sheppard urged women to vote for representatives who were 'truthful' in their speech and 'upright' in their dealings, and who lived 'cleanly' in their lives. There was no need for such men to be conventional, since what was 'conventionally right is often morally wrong'; witness those who, as a matter of convention, objected to women voting. The best political representatives would be committed to the well-being of the people rather than seeking self-aggrandisement; they would be guided by a 'true reverence for women' and a great love of country.[9]

Citizenship held out the possibility that women would no longer be understood as 'the sex' in contrast to men's fully human status. While women were expected to be chaste, 'impure men' could cause a girl's 'ruin'. For the women activists of the 1890s, sexuality was fraught with danger. The majority of young women, for example, worked as domestic servants and might fall prey to men's advances. Pregnancy meant instant dismissal and the loss of one's 'character', so vital for new employment. Married women faced the danger of dying in childbirth, which increased with successive pregnancies at a time when contraception was largely ineffectual. Syphilis was rife and women might be unknowingly infected, leading to miscarriages and debility.

Laws upheld different standards of behaviour in a variety of ways. The 1857 Divorce and Matrimonial Causes Act (which contained a double standard on adultery) and the Contagious Diseases Act of 1869 were weighted in men's favour. After the vote was won, activists worked hard to bring about reform of these laws and others — to raise the age of consent, for example, and to make incest a crime.

Sheppard was well aware that the eyes of the world were keenly following developments in New Zealand, just as the New Zealanders had followed women's progress elsewhere. She noted how congratulations had come from British suffragist Millicent Garrett Fawcett (whose hand signed my piece of ephemera) and from the American suffrage leader, Susan B. Anthony (whose name was given to a prize for women's history I was awarded in my American graduate school). Sheppard believed the educational task now extended beyond New Zealand's shores: to set an example that would assist suffrage movements elsewhere to achieve their goals. She thought of sending her now unneeded pamphlets and tracts to Tasmania or 'somewhere else where women are still working for the franchise'.[10]

Kate Sheppard concluded her 1893 report by pointing out that enfranchisement was a beginning, rather than an end. She lived to see the right to stand for Parliament extended to women in 1919, but by this time the political party system had hardened. The parties inhibited the impact of the democratic franchise by making candidates responsible more to the party, the leader and national issues than to the specific class or gender issues of the electors.[11] Political parties, were, in effect, men's clubs that succeeded in keeping women candidates out — as New Zealand's second woman lawyer, Ellen Melville, found out when she stood seven times, unsuccessfully, for Parliament.

It took 14 years, and as many attempts by women to be elected, after the passing of the Women's Parliamentary Rights Act in 1919 for the first woman, Elizabeth McCombs (Labour), to win an electorate. Her success in Lyttelton in September 1933 ocurred nearly 40 years to the day after women won the vote. Sheppard, by then 86 years old, may have been delighted that Christchurch was the first place to celebrate a woman Member of Parliament. As a consequence of McCombs' election, the 'No Women Permitted' sign over Bellamy's dining room in Parliament was removed, the wording of the swearing in was altered, and 'members' rather than 'gentlemen' now participated in the House. The fifth woman elected, Labour member Mabel Howard, served in Parliament for 26 years and became the first woman in Cabinet. Howard complained publicly, and to little avail, about parliamentary rules that disadvantaged women. She finally gained access to the use of a bathroom by threatening to climb out one window and into the bathroom via another in order to avoid the 'Gentlemen' sign on the door.

The boys' club atmosphere in Parliament continued into the 1980s, when the numbers of women doubled from a mere four in 1978 to eight in 1981. That boys' club had a significant impact on legislation. All four women members, for example, opposed the 1977 Contraception, Sterilisation and Abortion Bill, which went on to become law and tightened up access to abortion. A senior government MP's response to Mary Batchelor's 1980 question about the lack of representation of women at inter-governmental negotiations was to ask her who she slept with. The following year, Batchelor succeeded, supported by all the women in Parliament, in introducing a bill against domestic violence. In 1984 Annette King still found Parliament to be '*incredibly* sexist'.[12] And the numbers of women continued to rise at a snail's pace until the advent of MMP in 1996, to hover at around one-third in the 2000s. At the November 2017 election 46 women were elected to the New Zealand Parliament, making up an unprecedented 38.4 per cent of the total.

The women who signed the Suffrage Petition believed that their votes could help make New Zealand a better place for women and children. Their desire for the 'moral uplift of humanity' remains an inspiration, if interpreted very differently in the twenty-first century. The significant changes in the family, brought about by changing attitudes to divorce, the advent since the 1960s of highly effective contraception, and women's access to higher education and paid employment, could not be imagined in the 1890s. New medications led to effective treatments for venereal disease, but men became newly sensitised to sexual danger with the advent of AIDS in the 1980s. While the late nineteenth-century emphasis on chastity and self-control has faded, the #MeToo movement highlights contemporary concerns with sexual predation and harassment which were familiar to suffrage activists.

The first of the Christian commitments to 'God, Home and Humanity' that drove the WCTU has receded from public discourse to such an extent that in 2018 removing all religious references in the Parliamentary 'prayer' has been seriously discussed. For the women of the 1890s the church provided one of the few welcoming public places that propelled them into the world to create change. Christian denominations valued the work of women in the home and encouraged them to organise to spread religious values. In the Bible women found much to support their demands for a new moral order; 1 Corinthians 6:19–20, for example, provided language with which to argue for sexual restraint, speaking of the body as 'the temple of the Holy Ghost' and urging believers to 'glorify God in your body and in your spirit'. I think I could have paid more attention to the role of the church in my historical work. The fact that I have not says something about being raised in a church where I only ever heard men preach — and I often wanted to argue with them.

The religious commitment of the suffragists not only empowered women to work outside of the home, but also validated their work within it. While the women of the 1890s wanted to dignify domestic duties and take 'home values' of selflessness and caring into the world, 1970s feminists often saw the home as a prison to be escaped from and housework as drudgery. Today women still do the bulk of domestic work, even though they have escaped the 'prison' of home for the equally insistent demands of the labour force. And working lives are still organised around the male norm and take little account of family responsibilities.

The commitment to 'humanity', or the well-being of people collectively, still spurs political engagement. In 1899, Lucy Smith, associate editor of the WCTU journal *White Ribbon*, wrote: '[T]he New Zealand nation is the seedling, planted in beautiful soil, yet needing the watchful eye and the steady, skillful hand, that it may neither be blighted by the chill frosts of a selfish individualism, nor stunted by the fierce winds of materialism . . .'[13] In her first speech in Parliament as Labour leader in August 2017, Jacinda Ardern made clear her commitment to making New Zealand a better place for those living in poverty and without hope: a fairer place where all New Zealanders could access the best education, and obtain work and housing.[14] Her positive vision for equality in New Zealand led to an eventual Labour coalition government.

Continuities with the double standards of the 1890s remain. The day after she took on the Labour leadership, a radio show host claimed that the public should know Ardern's plans for having children, a question that she found 'totally unacceptable' in 2017 and one that was never asked of male candidates.[15] Kate Sheppard might never have imagined a 37-year-old, pregnant and unmarried woman as prime minister, but since she opposed acting merely out of convention (and herself lived in an unconventional household later in life) she might well applaud a national leader aspiring to demonstrate the compatibility between motherhood and political life, since fatherhood and political life have never been called into question.

Part of my motivation for my scholarly work is to honour the work of both Māori and Pākehā women who campaigned for women's rights in the past. They were courageous enough to speak out for the rights of women in the face of ridicule and the accusation that they would lose their feminine 'charms'. The women of the 1890s believed that their votes could help make New Zealand a better place for women and children. We don't have to live out all their dreams, but whatever our distance from them, making the world a better place remains a stellar aspiration.

1. Kate Sheppard, 'Hints to District Franchise Superintendents', *The Prohibitionist*, 27 February 1892, p. 3, reprinted in Margaret Lovell-Smith, *The Woman Question: Writings by the women who won the vote*. Auckland: New Women's Press, 1992, p. 72.

2. 'Ten Reasons Why the Women of New Zealand Should Vote', reprinted in ibid., p. 66.

3. Kate Sheppard, 'Address on the Subject of Woman Suffrage', reprinted in ibid., p. 67.

4. Cited in Judith Devaliant, *Kate Sheppard: A biography*. Auckland: Penguin Books, 1992, p. 124.

5. William Sidney Smith, *Outlines of the Women's Franchise Movement in New Zealand*. Christchurch: Whitcombe & Tombs, 1905, p. iii.

6. Kate Sheppard, 'Untitled Editorial', *White Ribbon*, July 1895, p. 1. Reprinted in Lovell-Smith 1992, p. 36.

7. Kate Sheppard, 'Suffrage Notes', *The Prohibitionist*, WCTU page, 16 July 1892, p. 3. Reprinted in ibid., p. 80.

8. Kate Sheppard, 'Hope Deferred', *The Prohibitionist*, WCTU page, 22 October 1892, p. 3. Reprinted in ibid., p. 82.

9. Kate Sheppard, 'To Women Voters', *The Prohibitionist*, WCTU page, 21 October 1893, p. 3. Reprinted in ibid., pp. 93–96.

10. Cited in Devaliant 1992, p. 121.

11. Carole Pateman, 'Three Questions about Womanhood Suffrage', in Caroline Daley and Melanie Nolan (eds), *Suffrage and Beyond: International feminist perspectives*. Auckland: Auckland University Press, 1994, pp. 343–44.

12. Denis Welch, *Helen Clark: A political life*. Auckland: Penguin Books, 2009, p. 98. Emphasis in the original.

13. *White Ribbon*, October 1899, p. 1.

14. Jacinda Ardern, speech in Parliament, 2 August 2017, accessed 29 January 2018, https://www.facebook.com/NZLabourParty/videos/10154873460186452/.

15. 'Totally unacceptable: New Zealand Labour leader Jacinda Ardern quizzed on baby plans', *Sydney Morning Herald*, 2 August 2017, accessed 29 January 2018, http://www.smh.com.au/world/totally-unacceptable-new-zealand-labour-leader-jacinda-ardern-quizzed-on-baby-plans-20170802-gxnj7z.html.

**SUE
BRADFORD**

LIVES
ON THE
LINE

TITLE:	Women's Social and Political Union Medal for Valour, awarded to Frances Parker
PRODUCTION:	Toye & Co., 1912
MATERIALS:	Silver, enamel, silk
DIMENSIONS:	42 (width) x 85 (height) x 8 (depth) x 22 (diameter) mm
CREDIT:	Purchased 2016
REGISTRATION:	GH024772

I've never been into medals. I grew up in a family where Dad's medals from the war were buried away somewhere and I never saw them until after he died. He didn't talk much about his years slogging through Italy, but when he did there was lots of swearing and sometimes he cried. He refused to join the RSA, and he and his medals were never on parade.

Partly as a result of this I grew up fascinated by war, and by peace, like so many of our post-World War Two generation. For me medals seemed to be about the glorification of war, not any kind of genuine acknowledgement of suffering and courage, although I understood why others felt differently.

When I was offered Frances Parker's medal as an object for this essay it felt quite alien. Suffrage medals? Yes, the achievement of women's suffrage was certainly a struggle worth honouring, but in such warlike terms? What was that about?

Then, of course, I began to look at the story behind the medal.

Frances Parker was born in Waimate in the Canterbury district in 1875. She came from a well-to-do family and was the niece of Lord Kitchener, a senior British army officer famous, among other things, for his role in setting up what became known as the world's first concentration camps during the Second Anglo-Boer War. When Frances was 22, Kitchener funded her to study at Cambridge University. After graduation she spent time working as a teacher in New Zealand and France before returning to the UK, where she became very active in the women's suffrage movement. By 1908 she was a member of the Women's Social and Political Union (WSPU), established by Emmeline Pankhurst and her daughters Christabel and Sylvia in 1903. Later on, Frances worked as a key organiser for the WSPU in Scotland and received the WSPU Medal for Valour in 1912.

Frances was first arrested on a suffragette action at Parliament in London in 1908 and sentenced to six weeks in prison. She went on to be arrested another four times, for activities including window smashing, arson and attempted arson. In July 1914, Frances and her friend Ethel Moorhead were charged with trying to set fire to Burns Cottage in Alloway, the first home of Robert Burns, Scotland's national poet. As part of a WSPU campaign to use hunger strikes as a strategic tool, Frances endured two lengthy periods as a hunger striker when imprisoned in 1912 and 1914. She was subjected to force-feeding, and, like some other women, was assaulted physically and sexually by female prison guards using methods nothing short of state-sanctioned torture.

After the worst of these incidents in 1914, Frances was sent from prison to a nursing home, from which she escaped. When war broke out in August that year, the WSPU suspended its militant actions and a general amnesty was offered to suffragettes. Frances volunteered her services for the war effort, becoming deputy controller of the Women's Army Auxiliary Corps in 1917. She was awarded a military medal, the Order of the British Empire. Frances died in 1924 aged 49, four years before women in the UK were granted full equal suffrage to men in 1928.

Frances bequeathed her WSPU Medal for Valour to her friend and fellow militant Ethel Moorhead. Ethel talked of Frances as having 'an exquisite madness — daring, joyous, vivid, strategic'.[1]

Around a thousand women were imprisoned during the campaign for women's suffrage in the UK. Besides the militant WSPU there were many other organisations using a variety of tactics to achieve the same goal New Zealand women had won a lot more peacefully some 35 years earlier.

I was shocked when I read a brief description, by Frances herself, of her ordeal in Perth Prison, Scotland. I don't want to reproduce her words here as I know that some find such details titillating, and even after all this time I feel our sister deserves some cloak of dignity. But having discovered a little of her story, I believe she deserved that medal — she and all the other women who received this acknowledgement for putting their lives on the line in order to obtain the same rights of political participation as those enjoyed by men. And after all, the WSPU was operating within the perceptions and practices of the era, co-opting the notion of medals to its own purpose, culture-jamming 1914-style to offer its own honour, deeply meaningful within the current societal norms.

In Aotearoa New Zealand 2018, time and geography separate us enormously from the realities of women's existence a hundred and more years ago. We can barely conceive how hard it was for women then to find even the slightest of freedoms in their everyday lives — in clothing, relationships, work and play as well as politics. For those who took part in the militant arm of the suffrage movement there must have been a sense of intense risk, commitment, solidarity and liberation. The extremity of some of their actions, including Emily Davison's sacrifice in throwing herself fatally in front of the King's horse at the 1913 Derby, must surely have been driven by an all-consuming desire for an emancipation that went far beyond women's right to vote.

The WSPU was the radical outlier of the movement for women's suffrage in Britain. Its members — most of whom were middle-class, comparatively well-off women — were criticised by some for their militant tactics, and by others for their focus on the vote rather than on much-needed social justice reforms. From August 1914, pacifist women left the organisation in disgust at the WSPU's support for Britain's entry into the war. Yet despite the splits and criticisms, the well-publicised activism of the union's pre-war years undoubtedly helped propel an unwilling male public and Parliament towards finally enacting universal suffrage.

I have been part of what I'd call the militant radical left of New Zealand street politics since the age of 15. I joined Auckland's Progressive Youth Movement in 1967 when still at school, terrified by the prospect of a nuclear holocaust destroying the planet and furious at New Zealand's support for the American war in Vietnam. I took part in demonstrations and other activities where we were unafraid to block streets, confront police or occupy buildings. There were activists who went further, blowing up buildings and flagstaffs and spending time in jail as a consequence. There was a sense, too, driven by the global wave of radical youth politics in the late '60s, that armed revolution could be just around the corner, and some were preparing for that as well.

Even as young people back then we knew we were continuing a tradition of militancy that didn't start in our generation, but which went back through time: for instance, the ongoing Māori struggles against colonisation, occupation and dispossession (at times meaning all-out war); the battles of employed workers for even the most basic of rights, from Blackball and Waihi through to the 1951 waterfront lockout and later; and the struggles of unemployed workers in the 1930s, which led to major riots.

Some of us took the lessons of the late '60s and early '70s into later struggles, perhaps most significantly the mobilisation against the 1981 Springbok tour. Prime Minister Rob Muldoon used the opportunity of an apartheid-era South African rugby tour to boost the election chances for his struggling National Party. He deliberately chose to plunge the country into a confrontation that for some of us on the front lines ended up feeling very close to civil war, and which also achieved the goal he was after: victory in the 1981 election.

I was a comparatively young footsoldier within the large anti-tour mobilisation group in Auckland. We met constantly to plan our next actions, with rugby matches and the concomitant protests taking place twice a week. One of the things that impressed me most was the group's willingness to support different levels of activity: from holding a cross and praying on a street corner and quiet marches with children and older folk, through to cat-and-mouse quasi-military street demos and independent small-group actions aimed at major disruption in towns and cities across the country. All these levels of activity were encouraged within a kaupapa of non-violent direct action and the clear common goal of stopping the tour.

Like others, I was arrested many times; we used mass arrest as a deliberate tactic. We took over the Waiatarua transmitter station, temporarily stopping the match broadcast one Saturday, and on another sunny afternoon raced through Auckland airport security to occupy an aircraft. Once I found myself caught up in what was almost a fixed battle between police and the Patu Squad at Kowhai School in Kingsland. Marx Jones and Grant Cole dropped flour bombs from a light aircraft at the final match: the protest air force in action.

I allude to these experiences only because I have come to realise that even politically interested younger people are not necessarily aware of what transpired in 1981. It's a long time ago now, and already unknown ancient history for some. Small wonder that many of us are oblivious to the experiences of the British suffragettes in 1908–14.

Tens of thousands of people had active involvement in the 1981 protests. And again, some of us took our experience forward into activism of the '80s and '90s: Māori organisations fighting against racism and for tino rangatiratanga; the development of the Pākehā treaty workers' movement; women's groups working on issues around pornography and sexism;

trade unions; the campaign for a nuclear-free New Zealand; the continuing struggle for unemployed workers' and beneficiaries' rights.

On the question of militancy, some of the lessons of 1981 which still resonate for me today are not only the reminder that we can and should respect all the levels of action that go into making up an effective activity or campaign, but also the insight that our solidarity from collective militant action can be a powerful force. Ordinary people, acting together, can make change. In the bravery, chaos and fear of collective direct action, we face down — even in what seems at times the feeblest of ways — the political and economic structures which hold all the power while we hold little or none.

Over the years, I have seen for myself how militancy can play a key role: for example, around the Vietnam War, the 1981 rugby tour, the nuclear-free campaign, and the many actions in support of greater Māori sovereignty. It is a great irony that so many of these campaigns ended up being retrospectively eulogised by later governments, even conservative ones. This, of course, is just what occurred in the decades following the achievement of universal women's suffrage in Britain, despite the use of militant tactics that at the time were shocking to so many.

The one movement in which I've been intensely involved that has never achieved such post-facto eulogising has been the fight by unemployed workers and beneficiaries for 'jobs, education and a living wage for all'. This, perhaps, is unsurprising, given that the economic struggle of the most dispossessed and despised in society directly confronts the capitalist system. Those without jobs often end up using militant tactics — because when you can't even withdraw your labour as employed workers can, you're left with no other option.

Some of us who have used militancy to effect change take care to ensure it is appropriate to the context; tactics that are excessive, or which are too far out of line with the opinion of those whose support we seek, can harm the cause. Frances Parker and her activist sisters engaged in a focused militancy that took their cause to the limits of what was sensible and possible in early twentieth-century Britain. In our groups, we analyse the situation and the political and economic forces at play. We consider the range of tactics possible, and whether there are other options better than militant action. And usually there are. But sometimes, when the time and situation call for it, we prepare — and act.

Beyond this brief reflection on the role of militancy in left activist politics, what might be taken from Frances Parker's story in respect of women's issues in Aotearoa New Zealand in 2018? We have come an enormously long way since full suffrage was achieved 125 years ago, but we still lack parity in political participation. Even though the current Parliament has the highest proportion of women MPs in history, with 48 women making up 40 per cent of our elected representation, this falls well short of the 50 per cent (or more) many of us would see as desirable. Women lag even further behind as a proportion of those elected to local government positions, apart from district health board membership.

And such statistics don't adequately reveal an even greater problem. Over many years of working with people who are among the most economically dispossessed in this country, I have come to realise that a basic ignorance of how our political system functions means another kind of dispossession is also at play here; it is expressed partly through high levels of non-voting at general elections, and partly through a sense of helplessness in the face of forces and systems that are simply incomprehensible.

Many young people grow to adulthood without any understanding of how Parliament, law-making and political parties work, nor of the deeper economic forces shaping society. This leaves them disenfranchised, with a sense that their vote and voice don't count. It is way past time basic political and economic literacy formed part of the core school curriculum. Alongside this, the voting age should be lowered to 16, so that people from all backgrounds can start life knowing that their opinion and experience matter. Once people are detached from the school system, it is much harder to help them learn that they, too, have a right to take a wider interest in the world around them, and that there are ways to change that world, from both inside and outside parliamentary processes.

This is not gender-specific, but in a year when we are celebrating 125 years since suffrage it is timely to remember those women who are most locked out of active involvement in political life. The example of the way in which Metiria Turei was vilified by media, public and politicians just prior to the 2017 election only serves to exacerbate the sense that it's hugely risky for women who don't come from the world of middle-class white privilege to step out into the terrifying exposure of mainstream political life.

Beyond this element of personal risk, another way in which women on the margins — and those who support them — are disproportionately excluded from political participation is through the current lack of any party or other political organisation that gives them adequate voice and opportunity for their inclusion and representation in the places of power. At the time of writing, there is no broad-based party working openly for transformational structural change to the colonising, patriarchal, neoliberal-capitalist polity in which we live. It is a form of disenfranchisement when we have no party for whom to mobilise, or vote. Establishing major new parties and organisations without the backing of existing wealth and power is difficult in the extreme. Yet despite the difficulties, I'd love to see an organisation driven by women and by low- and no-income workers and beneficiaries become a new and serious option for participation and the building of counterhegemonic power, inside and outside Parliament.

I'd like us to demonstrate more courage: not only in the street tactics we might use in support of a cause, but also in finding new ways of educating and mobilising for longer-term change on a kaupapa of genuine participation and for a country grounded in economic, social, Tiriti and ecological justice. Taking part in emancipatory organising and action is in itself a key to our liberation — not just through militancy and not just through voting, but as a means by which many more of us can work together to create a more hopeful future in these dangerous times.

The biggest inspiration I draw from the story of Frances Parker is in the quote from her friend Ethel: that she had 'an exquisite madness — daring, joyous, vivid, strategic'. That seems a fair summary of how it feels to put analytical, precise and collectively planned militancy into action.

1   Cited in Claire Regnault, 'International Women's Day: Suffrage for all', Te Papa Blog, 8 March 2016, accessed 13 April 2018, http://blog.tepapa.govt.nz/2016/03/08/international-womens-day-suffrage-for-all/.

**MORGAN
GODFERY**

OUR
COUNTRY'S
MIRROR

TITLE:	La Nouvelle Zélande
PRODUCTION:	Margaret Butler, 1938
MATERIALS:	Bronze
DIMENSIONS:	450 (width) x 550 (height) x 300 (depth) mm
CREDIT:	Gift of the Academy of Fine Arts, 1950
REGISTRATION:	1950-0016-9

TIME

Time, my family tells me, is music in motion. We measure our day against the clock's metronomic tick, and we dance to its daily rhythms. We wake, drink, eat, work, create and sleep. On our best days time's passing feels like a melody; we embrace every beat and delight in every pause. But on our worst days time is a cacophony — we wake, work, fight, eat, drink and we forget to sleep.

Our people order their time in songs and calls, because how else do you 'count the time'? Time itself begins with a dread scream as Papatūānuku's children sink their hands into her ashen flesh, ripping her from her lover. And each year begins with a soft cry — the sob, sob, sob of a son, Tāwhirimātea, who never left his mother. And each day begins in ritual trills, the high and low notes of a karakia tīmatanga. 'Whakataka te hau ki te uru.' Get ready for the westerly. 'Whakataka te hau ki te tonga.' And prepare for the southerly.

My relationship with time is nowhere near as imaginative, even if I can take comfort in its washed-out routine. The alarm whines at 6 a.m., and my accumulated habits take me through the day. My work looks much the same as it did the day before (unfinished), my menu remains more or less the same, and my eyes droop at the same time every night, as mechanical as the tick, tock of the bedroom clock. (Post)modernity promises thrilling adventures and instant reward — you can travel to any corner of the world with a click or an airfare, and with every tweet comes a heart — but our lives are as constrained by circumstance, whether economics or mere disposition, as those of our ancestors were constrained by seasons.

This is the paradox of our age: our lives are as determined as at any other point in the last half-century, and yet they are also more unstable and uncertain. Routine assumptions like 'a job for life' no longer hold and technology is transforming the way we live, learn and date. 'Ka mura, ka muri' — we walk backwards into the future, as the whakataukī goes. In other words, history is organising the world as we find it, and so we better pay attention to it. But capitalism and postmodernity reshape our relationship with the past. Today, time is in a hurry: tech-utopians predict imminent 'disruption'; politicians promise the 'innovation' that never quite arrived is finally here; and as soon as something appears — whether a switchboard operator or a train driver, MySpace or Bebo — it disappears.

The future is rushing forward, a tackle-line coming closer and closer to contact. From here it seems as if the only way to face is towards the future, nervously waiting for the crunch. Yet the thing we miss when we overlook the past is that how we live today — uncertainly, if sometimes monotonously, or, as literary critic Fredric Jameson put it, in a 'paradox' between 'an unparalleled rate of change on all the levels of social life and an unparalleled standardization of everything'[1] — is not necessarily The Natural Order of Things. After all, not even Papatūānuku and Ranginui were together forever. Time is not linear, racing from ignorance to enlightenment, and so the present is not necessarily just or desirable simply because it is the present.

In Papua New Guinea the Yupno community point to

the river mouth when discussing the past and towards its mountainous source when discussing the future, a pattern of thought exactly reversing our customary understanding of time and its flow. Ka mura, ka muri. We walk backwards into the future. And so it sometimes is in art, where the social distinctions between then, now and what may come melt away in the encounter. Not in the affected sense in which time stops when you encounter a classic, as if all of the universe stood to attention, but in the sense that art can reshape our perspective on history, politics and what it means to inhabit the here and now. Romantics often talk about art as an 'escape'. The encounter happens within its own self-contained world. But instead of a reprieve from history, politics and our own time, art is a way of getting another angle of vision on how each shapes social life.

In other words, history and politics are written as vividly in art as they are in books and laws. This is as true for Hotere's furious *Polaris* as it is for Warhol's pop politics; as true for Banksy's street kitsch as it is for Peter Robinson's cutting *Boy Am I Scared Eh!*

Sculpture, in particular, can capture and reflect the moment we inhabit, its durability and definiteness (as well as its fragility). In *La Nouvelle Zélande* (1938) Margaret Butler, the sculptor Lord Bledisloe once called 'our local lady Praxiteles',[2] urges us to consider just what it means to embody the nation in a sculpture of a Māori woman.

PLACE

'**He manu hou ahau, he pī ka rere.**' I am like a fledgling, a newborn bird just learning to fly, whispered Te Mautaranui. They were the final words of a Ngāti Awa chief who understood a lifetime is never long enough. In Te Mautaranui's world men are never permanent. Only women are forever. The human story begins with Hineahuone, the woman who sprang from the soil, and it ends with Hinenuitepō, the goddess guarding the threshold between life and death, and who crushed an immortality-seeking Māui between her cosmic thighs.

In te ao Māori women are the beginning and end of time. Miriama Heketa — Butler's subject, the heavy-eyed matriarch of the Ngāti Pōneke Young Māori Club, the Wellington-based cultural club named by Sir Āpirana Ngata — understood as much. Heketa modelled for *La Nouvelle Zélande* as well as Butler's other masterpiece, the *Maori Madonna* (1937–39). In her first act Heketa is Hineahuone — a kind of non-biblical Eve — and the personification of the nation: *Nouvelle Zélande;* New Zealand. In her second act Heketa is reborn as Mary, the Queen of Heaven, Christianity's own Hinenuitepō.

'He ao, he ao,' roared Hine-te-Apārangi. A cloud! After months at sea hunting Muturangi's demonic octopus, Hine-te-Apārangi, her husband Kupe and their crew crash against the dunes. 'So the stories are true,' Kupe says, sinking his feet into the Hokianga's red-hot sand. 'Māui did haul land from the sea.' In the colonial telling Kupe 'rediscovers' New Zealand. But in truth a woman called Aotearoa into existence. 'He ao, he ao,' roared Hine-te-Apārangi, not Kupe or their crew.

'Kia whakatāne ake au i ahau!' Let me act like a man, Wairaka cries, dashing across the shoreline. In every heave and wheeze are the memories of her island home: the rolling waters, the tang of salt, the steaming mountains, and the suffocating heat. In the traditional telling the current is dragging the Mātaatua, the ancient waka that carried Wairaka and her people from Hawaiki to New Zealand, towards the white caps at the Whakatāne river mouth. Wairaka, all legs and arms, lowers the sail, lifts a paddle and steers her people's last connection to home to safety.

At every moment in this country's history — from its founding during Hine-te-Apārangi's time, its settlement during Wairaka's time, and its recent history in Miriama Heketa's time — women are at the very centre of social life. And yet they are rarely at the centre of politics or art. This is the genius of *La Nouvelle Zélande*. Butler returns Māori women to the very centre of this country's story. Heketa is Hine-te-Apārangi and she is Wairaka. She is Hineahuone and Hinenuitepō. She is *New Zealand*.

And yet perhaps all of this is asking too much, a critic might insist, because Butler's bronze bust is stultifyingly conventional. Personifying the country in a 'symbolic female' is nothing new. This is style rather than statement, and the piece's simplicity — its clean lines, its symmetry — might warn against interpretivism. After all, this is the same artist who 'won "orientalist" acclaim' for *Head of an Arab* (1927),[3] the sort of romantic sculpture mourning the descent of the subject's world (the East) and celebrating the ascent of the artist's (the West).

In short, Butler is not innocent, let alone a guilt-ridden Pākehā with a pro-Māori agenda.

Or so the argument goes. But Butler is not necessarily asking audiences to impute her work with intention or interrogate her political commitments. Instead she is asking audiences to re-orient themselves: What would it mean to understand the country as Māori women do? In *La Nouvelle Zélande* Heketa is not simply one part of the nation, her own discrete person in her own turbulent time. She *is* the nation. Then, now, and in the future. What is at stake in *La Nouvelle Zélande* is a way of seeing.

You might call this the old-fashioned gaze. '[C]inematic codes create a gaze, a world, and an object, thereby producing an illusion cut to the measure of desire,' wrote feminist film theorist Laura Mulvey, outlining how mainstream films exploit and encourage patriarchal ways of seeing.[4] We might repurpose this insight for sculpture as well, and then applaud Butler's neat reversal. In Heketa, Butler is proposing another angle of vision. *La Nouvelle Zélande* is asking what it might mean to look upon the country not as men do but as *Māori women* do.

This must make spectators uncomfortable. The average Māori woman will live a shorter, more insecure life than the average Pākehā. At work, Pākehā women earn between $3 and $6 more per hour than their Māori colleagues, as if tangata whenua were twice-crippled: first with a vagina, and then with brown skin. 'The root cause of the gulf in wages is colonisation and capitalism,' writes Tainui waka's Miriama Aoake.[5] From a Māori perspective ours is not the 'God's Own Country' of Richard Seddon's imagination.

But maybe this is too gloom-ridden. Everyone acknowledges that things are not precisely the same as in Heketa's day: te reo Māori is an official language; a bloke from Ngāti Wai is deputy prime minister; and even Tame Iti is a national treasure. From here it might seem as if we — as in Māori — are emancipated. Our lives are our own, and we are no longer subjects of empire or dominion. But if this is true, what kind of world were we emancipated into?

The answer seems obvious, but it is worth stating for the record: one where the political economy, social relations, and distribution of benefits and burdens remain more or less the same now as they were half a century ago. We still earn less and die younger. This is not the same country that, say, former prime minister John Key would identify. One imagines that, for Key, capitalism and colonialism are synonymous with progress rather than misery. 'Māori probably acknowledge that settlers had a place to play and brought with them a lot of skills and a lot of capital,' Key remarked in 2014.[6]

This is why perspective matters. And this is why *La Nouvelle Zélande* matters. If we understand the world not only as Heketa might, but also as Māori women might, we acquire another angle of vision on the same social facts: the gender pay gap is an injustice, but it is a double injustice for Māori women, for example. Tangata whenua share New Zealand with tangata tiriti, but we understand and experience our country in different ways.

THE ARTIST

'**Time is a river** which sweeps me along, but I am the river,' wrote Jorge Luis Borges, the Argentine poet and intellectual, arguing that time is an illusion. 'It is a tiger which destroys me, but I am the tiger; it is a fire which consumes me, but I am the fire.' For Borges, time is not something that happens to us. Rather, we are time, and so there is no one single time 'in which all things are linked as in a chain'. Instead, experiences — of 'fires, wars, epidemics' — are 'multiplied in many mirrors', meaning we each come at time, place and events differently.[7]

La Nouvelle Zélande is our country's mirror. Not that many people saw it that way. Margaret Butler remained more or less invisible throughout her life. Born in Greymouth in 1884, she spent most of her childhood in Wellington, and then her most productive years in Europe from 1923 to 1934, exhibiting in London, Paris and other parts of the continent in that uncertain interval between world wars. Ill health would force Butler home — from birth she was club-footed, often encountering physical limitations — where she would go on to sculpt *La Nouvelle Zélande*.

And yet for all of her frightening talent the painters Frances Hodgkins and Mabel Hill were better known at home. Fellow sculptor Francis Shurrock had greater reach. Even after her death in 1947 Butler did not become a national treasure, a local El Greco. '[Margaret Butler] analyses with penetration all the types of humanity that she portrays,' François Thiébault-Sisson, a French art critic, enthused.[8] But most New Zealanders did not seem to know any better, even if the then prime minister Peter

Fraser was one of the famous mourners at Butler's funeral.

Perhaps this is because sculptors were sometimes ridiculed as mere craftspeople. Butler studied at Wellington 'Technical' School. Or perhaps a petty politics of some kind is at play. But in this year, 125 years after New Zealand women struggled for and won the vote, it seems appropriate to reclaim, re-examine and appreciate again Butler's body of work. Not necessarily because she is or should be a feminist icon but because her work urges us to re-examine our own country. *La Nouvelle Zélande*, embodying the nation in Heketa, a Māori woman, encourages us to look at New Zealand not as those with power or comfort would but as those without would. This is Butler's genius. *La Nouvelle Zélande* is our country's mirror. The question is, who is looking back?

---

1   Fredric Jameson, *The Seeds of Time*. New York: Columbia University Press, 1996, p. 15. Jameson is an American literary critic and Marxist theorist, perhaps best known for his analysis of postmodernity and capitalism.

2   Cited in Mark Stocker, 'Butler, Margaret Mary', *Dictionary of New Zealand Biography*, first published in 1998. Te Ara — the Encyclopedia of New Zealand, accessed 12 December 2017, https://teara.govt.nz/en/biographies/4b55/butler-margaret-mary.

3   Mark Stocker, 'Margaret Butler: An invisible sculptor?', Te Papa Blog, 14 March 2016, accessed 12 December 2017, http://blog.tepapa.govt.nz/2016/03/14/margaret-butler-an-invisible-sculptor/.

4   Laura Mulvey, 'Visual Pleasures and Narrative Cinema', first published in *Screen*, vol. 16, issue 3 (1975), pp. 6–18, accessed 12 December 2017, https://www.sas.upenn.edu/~cavitch/pdf-library/Mulvey_%20Visual%20Pleasure.pdf.

5   Miriama Aoake, 'Pay Equity in New Zealand is a Race Issue, Not Just a Gender Issue', *VICE NZ*, 8 March 2017, accessed 12 December 2017, https://www.vice.com/en_nz/article/5343eb/pay-equity-in-new-zealand-is-a-race-issue-not-just-a-gender-issue.

6   'New Zealand "settled peacefully" — PM', *Stuff*, 20 November 2014, accessed 12 December 2017, https://www.stuff.co.nz/national/politics/63377474/new-zealand-settled-peacefully-pm.

7   Maria Popova, 'A New Refutation of Time: Borges on the most paradoxical dimension of existence', *Brain Pickings*, 19 September 2016, accessed 12 December 2017, https://www.brainpickings.org/2016/09/19/a-new-refutation-of-time-borges/.

8   Stocker, 2016.

**SANDRA
CONEY**

UNFINISHED BUSINESS

TITLE:	Single 3c gummed stamp, first day cover, '75th Anniversary Universal Suffrage'
PRODUCTION:	New Zealand Post, 1968
MATERIALS:	Paper, ink
DIMENSIONS:	26 (width) x 30 (height) mm
CREDIT:	Gift of Russell Close in the name of his mother, Mildred Close, 2016
REGISTRATION:	PH001661

The centenary of women's suffrage in New Zealand was celebrated in 1993 with a cornucopia of memorial projects — sculptures were unveiled, historic petitions digitised, television series and books were launched. The seventy-fifth anniversary in 1968 was marked with something much more modest — a stamp.

And what a curious stamp it is. A disembodied man's arm is poised in the act of dropping a ballot paper in a box. Matching his, a woman's arm is suspended doing the same thing. We know one is a man and one is a woman by their dress: his arm has a suit cuff and her bare arm is adorned with a bracelet. How easy it was in 1968 to convey sexual identity by fragments of dress. Thus the image economically conveys the theme of the stamp: the celebration of three-quarters of a century of universal suffrage.

Women's long campaign to win the vote — a campaign that did not resort to the violent protest of our British sisters, but was prolonged and intense nonetheless — is neatly subsumed under the wider issue of votes for everyone, achieved of course by the female suffrage, at which point New Zealand women caught up with Pākehā and Māori men.

Such an image, redolent of order and calm, belies the intensity and sacrifice of the New Zealand suffrage campaign. Women experienced disappointment, abuse and opposition, to say nothing of the opportunity costs of the campaign. They grew middle-aged and old fighting this campaign, when they could have been doing other things, things their brothers, at least the Pākehā ones, could then parade as male-only achievements — mountains climbed, bridges built, business fortunes made.

Of course, women's struggle for equality was not over with the achievement of the vote. In the course of those next 75 years, women's time was also consumed by the fight to gain the right to stand for Parliament, to serve on juries and to work while married, for reproductive rights, equal pay and a long list of other opportunities that were far from complete in 1968. Over that time, New Zealand had experienced two world wars and the Great Depression, periods of history during which it was hard to argue for women's rights, though some continued to do so.

Yes, 1968 was a quiet year for women's rights, though it was a calm that belied the ferment brewing underneath.

My own life was on that cusp between a fairly traditional woman's life and a break for freedom. Like others of my generation I benefited from the education available to girls after World War Two, though I was oblivious to the fact that we girls in academic schools were being groomed, at the behest of government, for service in schools and hospitals.

I completed one year at teachers' college and university before marrying at the age of 18. I had a child before my nineteenth birthday. My life course was a common one at the time. In the era of the stamp, nearly half of all brides were under 21 years of age — 455 in every 1000 in 1966 — and a quarter of first births were to women under 20 years.[1] In 1966, motivated by a desire to be able to support myself should anything happen to my husband — I have no idea where this ambition came from, except a precept drummed into me growing up, that the worst thing that could happen to you was to have no money — I re-enrolled at university. My husband got a job as an accountant at the steel mill at Waiuku and we went to live in deepest suburbia in Papakura.

My son started primary school in 1968 and I was on the school committee. I found out at the first meeting that I and the one other woman in the group were expected to take turns bringing freshly baked scones to committee meetings for supper. I attended weekly sewing bees for the mothers, making items for the school fair, where we addressed each other as Mrs Coney and so on, never reaching the intimacy of first names. We were defined by our husbands. I was regarded as very peculiar as I was going to university and because of my clothes. I had taken to the new mini styles and regularly sewed up racy little numbers with minimal amounts of fabric.

Papakura was a long way to go to university, especially on the bus. My husband was a progressive sort — believe me, thousands of husbands wouldn't have been — and supported this. At university, I read in the student newspaper *Craccum* that a number of other mothers on campus were thinking of starting a crèche. I went to the students' association office and got the contact details.

There were mothers who were staff members like Judith Bassett and Nadja Tollemache; wives of staff members, like Nancy Bonham; and other student mothers such as Sharleen Forbes and Miriam Jackson (later Saphira). We formed the Student and Staff Nursery Society and went about setting up a crèche. What a relief it was to meet other women whose horizons extended beyond the home. I had had a bit of a feminist epiphany one day when, looking out of my kitchen window, I observed the woman across the road — whom I very rarely saw outside her house — emerge from her property, with a hat on, in her best dress and with a handbag swinging from her arm. She held, straight out in front of her, a plate with a cloth over it. She was on her way to a morning tea. I watched her and thought, I've got to get out of this.

As a young woman I had been brought up in an all-girl family where my father used to complain good-humouredly about living in 'a house full of women'. This conveyed a certain illusion of power on the part of my sister and mother, as in the outside world my father was a very powerful man, a local body politician and leader of the rugby union. We were brought up expected to do anything boys and men did, intellectually and physically. My father challenged us to do even the most risky things by calling us, if we hesitated, 'windy'. We surfed in the biggest surf, swam the harbour, argued about history, and had no idea how to cook or clean. Consequently, the prejudice and obstacles the Student and Staff Nursery Society encountered from the university authorities, and even from the students' association itself, came as a complete surprise to me.

When university council members told us we had to choose between motherhood and education I was incredulous. What I soon realised was that along with the prejudice came the power to withhold from us any help in the way of premises, funding or resources. Dorothy Winstone earned my lifelong respect for her efforts to support us: as the only woman on the university council she could do only so much to counteract the prevailing disapproval. The students' association was not much better, but offered cleaning products and toilet paper. On the home front, my mother-in-law chastised me for participating in an *Auckland Star* article about our efforts to start the crèche. I was told my married surname was not mine to broadcast and that a lady only had her name in the paper when she was born, married and died.

Before the crèche experience I had come across some feminist texts, principally *The Second Sex* (1949) by Simone de Beauvoir and Betty Friedan's *The Feminine Mystique* (1963), but the great flood of books that was generated by the women's liberation movement was yet to come. The first commercial edition of Valerie Solanas's *SCUM Manifesto* appeared in 1968, but I do not think I read it until a couple of years later. For me, it was the new breed of feminist novels which set me thinking: books like Doris Lessing's *Martha Quest* (1952) and the *Children of Violence* series, and particularly Margaret Drabble's *The Millstone* (1965), which I read serialised in a groundbreaking British women's magazine called *Nova*. Closer to home, in 1968 Marcia Russell founded the wonderful *Thursday*, a mainstream magazine covering a wide range of feminist topics from suburban neurosis to abortion. It once featured Angela Davis on its cover! Think of that!

The *New Zealand Woman's Weekly* was generally in the

traditional women's magazine mould, except that it featured a columnist, Cherry Raymond, who wrote about risky topics like menopause and abortion. Raymond also broke new ground for women journalists with her penetrating IYA radio interviews. The programme was annoyingly labelled *Feminine Viewpoint* — such titles were a pervasive form of segregation by which women's voices were pigeonholed. What these new publications and media had in common was questioning the expected life course for educated women and beginning a powerful critique of the female domestic role, which eventually would prove unstoppable.

The plethora of feminist organisations of the 1970s also lay in the wings, and it was the more traditional women's organisations that provided a feminist voice. Although the National Organization for Women was formed in the US in 1966, there was nothing similar in New Zealand. Older organisations such as the National Council of Women, the Council for Equal Pay and Opportunity and the Young Women's Christian Association spoke for women in these years. The newly formed Society for Research on Women led workshops for Playcentre mothers on the changing role of women, their publication surprisingly emblazoned with the iconography of a woman breaking her chains.[2] Psychiatrists from the mental hospitals stepped up to warn women of the perils of suburban life.

It is not surprising, then, that if you go to the major newspapers on the seventy-fifth anniversary of women's suffrage, which the stamp commemorates — 19 September 1968 — you will find that women's achievement is not mentioned.

This was in the middle of the local body election campaign, and Dove-Myer Robinson (Robbie) was campaigning for the Auckland mayoralty with slogans that could come from today, such as 'Hold the rates!' and 'Expanding Auckland!'[3]

Headlines of the day declared 'Vietcong flee as Anzacs go into action' and 'George Wallace promises guns for all', while in the 'Women's World' section a housewife could learn how 'You and a leg of mutton can create infinite variety' and that the British Medical Association, Wilson & Horton and the National Marriage Guidance Council had collaborated on a new handbook called *Getting Married*. The only remotely serious item for women was an article about how Iranian women were moving into 'what we usually regard as masculine professions', a reminder that the Middle East was on a more liberal trajectory 50 years ago than now.[4]

Employment was deeply gendered at the time, and the job vacancy advertisements reflected this. Some advertisements were headed simply 'Male clerk' or, even more baldly, 'Man'. Businesses seeking receptionists asked for 'Young lady, approximately 16 years old, with pleasant personality'. 'Pleasant personality' and 'tidy appearance' were much more sought-after qualifications for women than anything more formal.

Later, in 1973, I analysed all those frightful advertisements for my part in a submission on behalf of Auckland Women's Liberation to the Select Committee on Women's Rights.[5] Over two years the committee heard submissions on discrimination against women. This led to the Human Rights Commission Act 1977. Perhaps I can take a bit of credit for it becoming illegal to even mention gender in job adverts. A friend also recently pointed out to me that the prohibition on requiring the age of job applicants or being able to specify the age of applicants — banned by the Human Rights Act 1993 — explains New Zealand's exceptionally high rate of older working people compared to much of the rest of the world.

If sexual equality was invisible in the media in 1968, racial equality was not doing much better. There were at this time no Treaty of Waitangi protests and the radical groups like Ngā Tamatoa that emerged in the early 1970s did not exist. It was mainly the establishment groups such as the churches and Māori Council (and students), rather than any young activists, that had protested the all-white All Black tour of South Africa in 1960. In 1967 the New Zealand Rugby Union had declined to send another all-white team to South Africa, but that battle was far from won. Despite the United Nations, in 1968, calling for a sporting boycott of South Africa, in 1970 New Zealand toured that country with Māori deemed 'honorary whites'. In 1981 the country erupted when South Africa sent a segregated team to New Zealand.

Even so, there was often greater awareness of racism overseas than in New Zealand's own backyard. On Suffrage Day 1968, the *New Zealand Herald* reported a rather shameful episode in New Zealand race relations when the Northern Māori Labour MP Matiu Rata tried to get Parliament to support his motion to have a broadcasting matter returned to the Māori Affairs Committee for reconsideration.

Rata had petitioned Parliament to compel the Broadcasting

Corporation to adopt correct pronunciation for Māori place names and it had declined to do anything. Now he told Parliament: 'It is one thing for members of the public to choose how they pronounce names: it is another for a public authority in this country to interfere deliberately with a language spoken by more than 100,000 people in this country.'[6]

His motion was defeated on a voice vote. Rata would go on to found the Waitangi Tribunal, as Minister of Māori Affairs in the Third Labour Government; later, disenchanted with Labour, he founded the Mana Motuhake Party. He is another outstanding figure in New Zealand's history, who, like those feminist foremothers, spent his life working for freedoms that those with all the freedoms took for granted. How much more might Rata have achieved had he been born onto a level playing field?

Superficially, New Zealand paraded that it was doing nicely in race relations. All the legal discriminations had been removed, but not the structural consequences of colonisation. The claim of universal equality implied by that immaculately suited brown arm dropping the voting paper in the ballot box was a fiction. The 1968 *Yearbook* tells us that life expectancy was 69.17 for non-Māori men and 74.75 for non-Māori women. For Māori the figures were 59.05 for men and 61.37 for women, a gap of over a decade. Infant mortality was 16.13 per 1000 live births for non-Māori and 28.03 for Māori.[7]

The imminent social and political movement that would revolutionise women's lives had its parallel for Māori. Influenced by international civil and political rights movements, new, more confrontational methods were on the horizon and would play out at Bastion Point, Waitangi and Raglan, and on rugby fields and indeed the length and breadth of New Zealand.

Postwar New Zealand was a prosperous social democracy that — unlike much of the world today — provided the preconditions for challenges to the prevailing order. Everyone had access to free education, even at tertiary level, and free health care. Unemployment was nearly unheard of (141 unemployment benefits paid in 1968) and there were universal supports for families (66,816 family benefits were paid).[8] Yes, there were many battles to be fought, but it was safe to raise them, and the young, educated postwar generation knew about social movements overseas and were rearing to go.

Underlying the apparent calm of 1968 a veritable storm was brewing that would challenge all aspects of New Zealand life.

A second stamp, commemorating 20 years since the passing of the UN Universal Declaration of Human Rights (UDHR) in 1948, was issued with the suffrage stamp. Nineteen sixty-eight was deemed International Year for Human Rights, which makes the reaction to Rata all the more extraordinary. It was fitting that these two stamps were a pair, as women's rights are human rights, but the link was not explicitly made at the time, and even today is often not made. What women were doing was not seen as part of a wider struggle by indigenous peoples, Afro-Americans, workers, youth and so on. Certainly this was a connection made by the principal author of the UDHR, the totally admirable

Eleanor Roosevelt, who never shirked from sticking her neck out for the underdog and is really the progenitor of all our human rights advances of the past 70 years. Roosevelt used her power as former First Lady to challenge discrimination and significantly advance the rights of oppressed groups in a way that no First Lady since has come near.[9]

New Zealand, alongside a number of other small countries, can take a bow for helping ensure that the newly formed United Nations had a strong focus on human rights and that the scope of human rights was broad. In 1946, at a meeting in San Francisco to advance planning for the UN, our prime minister, Peter Fraser, argued that the UN principles should include that 'all members of the organisation undertake to preserve, protect and promote human rights and fundamental freedoms, and in particular the rights of freedom from want, freedom from fear, freedom of speech, and freedom of worship'. These principles eventually appeared in the UN Charter, Article 55: 'universal respect for, and observance of, human rights and fundamental freedoms for all without distinction as to race, sex, language, or religion'.

Against the prevailing view of Western nations, New Zealand was a strong proponent of the argument that civil and political rights should be accompanied by social, cultural and economic rights, a position shared by Eleanor Roosevelt. We can be proud that Fraser argued this position and that our country's case was put to the UN by a woman, Ann Newlands, President of the Women's Section of the Labour Party. Now there's a woman's name I had never heard of before and a new foremother to celebrate.

New Zealand's position remains as relevant today as in 1948. One of the New Zealand delegation back then, Dr Colin Aikman, a young lawyer whose role it was to advise Newlands, argued cogently:

> Experience in New Zealand has taught us that the assertion of the right of personal freedom is incomplete unless it is related to the social and economic rights of the common man. There can be no difference of opinion as to the tyranny of privation and want. There is no dictator more terrible than hunger.[10]

These words echo down the decades as a rebuke. In 2018, the World Economic Forum heard from Oxfam that the richest 1 per cent of New Zealanders captured 28 per cent of the wealth created in the previous year, while the 1.4 million people making up the country's poorest 30 per cent barely got 1 per cent.[11] The Oxfam report makes the point that women's economic equality (and, indeed, any kind of fair distribution of wealth) will never be gained under the prevailing economic order. Today, 70 years after the UDHR, closing the pay gap for New Zealand women remains unfinished business. And while it is important to celebrate the gains depicted on those 1968 stamps, it is astounding that today so much has still to be sorted for women and all New Zealand people. Half a century ago, New Zealand was an egalitarian nation that celebrated its egalitarianism. Yes, there was work waiting to be done, but there has been enormous slippage in the intervening years in areas where we had made gains. New Zealanders' civil and political rights are intact and well protected, but those social, cultural and economic rights have been seriously eroded by the years of neoliberalism. We could begin by including them in New Zealand's revision of its own Bill of Rights.

There is a big job ahead of us, but 2018 seems a very good year to start the mahi.

---

1   Department of Statistics, *New Zealand Official Yearbook 1968*. Wellington: Government Printer, 1968.

2   Society for Research on Women in New Zealand and Wellington Playcentre Association, *The Changing Role of Women*. Wellington: SROW, 1966.

3   Robinson had already been mayor, but was defeated in 1965 by R. G. McElroy. He won the 1968 election by 6000 votes.

4   *New Zealand Herald*, 19 September 1968.

5   See Women's Rights Committee, *The Role of Women in New Zealand Society: Report of the Select Committee on Women's Rights June 1975*. Wellington: Government Printer, 1975.

6   *New Zealand Herald*, 19 September 1968, p. 3.

7   Department of Statistics 1968.

8   Ibid.

9   Eleanor Roosevelt did much of her work after her husband's death, when President Truman appointed her to represent the US at the UN table.

10 Human Rights Commission, accessed 23 January 2018, https://www.hrc.co.nz/your-rights/human-rights/international-human-rights-legislation/universal-declaration-human-rights/#new-zealands-contribution-to-the-development-of-human-rights.

11 Oxfam NZ, 'Richest 1% of Kiwis bagged 28% of all wealth created last year', accessed 23 January 2017, https://www.oxfam.org.nz/news/richest-1-kiwis-bagged-28-all-wealth-created-last-year.

FIONA KIDMAN

PLAYING WITH FIRE

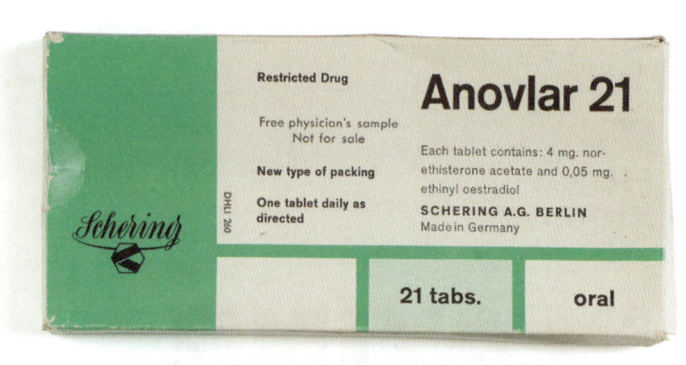

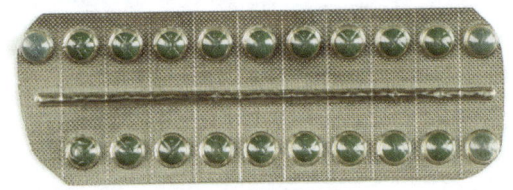

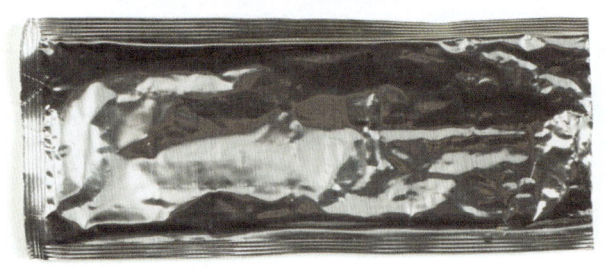

TITLE:	Anovlar 21 contraceptive pill
PRODUCTION:	Schering AG, circa 1965
MATERIALS:	Paper, cardboard, foil, plastic, hormone
DIMENSIONS:	173 (width) x 55 (height) x 15 (depth) mm
CREDIT:	Gift of Dame Margaret Sparrow, 2011
REGISTRATION:	GH022147

One day when I was a child my mother suggested I tidy the top of her dressing table. It was a plain deal piece of furniture crammed in the corner of the partitioned-off area of an old army hut that my parents called their bedroom. There wasn't much on it: a lipstick, a box of Coty face powder, some hair clips, a few bills. I soon got bored so I opened the top drawer. Inside was a little rectangular box, and inside that were some capsules that looked like brown jelly. I can't remember whether some were wrapped up or not; perhaps they were, but certainly some were exposed. I took them to my mother and asked her if they were lollies. She snatched them from my hand and said that I must never, never touch these again. It occurred to me later that, every now and then, a packet of about the same size would arrive in the mail and that the package wouldn't be opened in my presence.

They were, of course, contraceptive pessaries, something I would later, briefly, use to control my own fertility. Indeed, my mother slid me a packet on the eve of my wedding. I found them disgusting. They may have been Rendell's pessaries, although I think the packaging was the wrong colour. These definitely came in a black box.

All of this is by way of saying that my first encounters with reproductive control were tinged with the belief that something illicit was going on, not talked about, and certainly not a topic for unmarried women. A prudishness was evolving in the late 1940s that burst into full incandescent bloom in the 1950s. It's well documented that women developed new freedoms during World War Two, as they managed independent lives, did war work and brought up children on their own while fathers served in the forces. They had emerged from the shadows, and when men returned women were put back in their place behind their aprons. The kinder side of me thinks that it was not so much authoritarianism, or not all of it, as a primal urge to regenerate the species. All the same, as we wartime children arrived at our teen years, it made for lives that were hidden from our parents, hypocritical double standards, and worse, a reiteration of them when we ourselves married. The status quo had to be maintained. Yet we teenagers had had glimpses of freedom and seemingly forbidden fruits, particularly those of us who frequented dance halls and the rock'n'roll scene.

When I was seventeen I fell in love with a man with whom I had frequent pleasurable sex. We fell into bed whenever we could, usually without precautions. I remember the day he said to me: 'We're playing with fire, aren't we?' He meant, of course, that I might get pregnant. It was fine by him because he was planning to marry me anyway. He had already proposed.

Not long after, I fell out of love with him, and in love with someone else. But by that time, I was cautious. I had had a narrow escape, and by now the consequences of such abandon had been brought home to me. Friends got married in a hurry, or in their parents' front rooms with the minimum of witnesses. Young women disappeared for months at a time, and when they returned they were instinctively shunned. Older couples, if a girl was lucky, appeared to have impossibly late babies who grew up as the girl's sibling. At least the child stayed in the family, but most did not. Not only was the unmarried mother

PLAYING WITH FIRE

avoided, but she also wore a look of profound shock, as if she were in mourning. A close friend of the Roman Catholic faith told me that she had 'sinned' with the boy she really loved, and that they had broken up because the temptation to 'sin' again was so great.

And then, of course, there was abortion. I didn't know much about that or how women went about having them. They were illegal. The images described in an underground way suggested some sort of active charnel house awash with blood, overseen by a manic baby murderer. Later, I came to understand that a doctor of my acquaintance, who was a gentle, civil man, had 'helped out' some girls in our town in the orderly surroundings of his general practice; but he was the exception rather than the rule, and perhaps his reputation suffered a little as a result. But I also knew about a girl who had died after visiting another abortionist. And a friend had a botched abortion that rendered her sterile for the rest of her life.

Terror, that's what it was. We lived in terror. Our bodies were ready for sex whether or not we had yet to find the right mate, but, back then, in the 1950s, the results could deliver shame and grief in equal measure, possible rejection by our parents, the lonely desperate giving of birth in cruel and unfeeling surroundings, the loss of children, bitterness and shame. The results have followed generations of people in search of their birth parents, and for many it's still an unresolved issue.

My own out-of-wedlock pregnancy scare was, in the end, just that, but it hastened the date of my marriage, one that would endure for the next 57 years, the right mate as it turned out. I got lucky. But we didn't have two beans to rub together, as the saying goes, and we were not ready for a baby. The doctor frowned on hearing this. It would be best, he thought, if I were to get on with things. I was twenty and healthy, after all. He reluctantly fitted me for a diaphragm. It probably wouldn't have made much difference; after I gave birth a couple of years later, I never conceived a lasting pregnancy again. Something had gone wrong, but I wasn't to know it then. I was still seeking birth control when someone mentioned at a coffee morning that there was a pill to stop one from getting pregnant. 'Coffee mornings' were a euphemism for local mothers getting together while the children were at kindergarten and telling each other all about their lives.

We dressed up for these occasions in twinsets and pearl necklaces. Ideally, most of us wanted two children, although three were fine if they were spaced enough for us to catch our breath between pregnancies. It was the mid-1960s, we stayed home and looked after children, there was disapproval of women who worked outside of home (though I managed to break the mould somewhat by working from inside the home), we admired the whiteness of each others' napkins on the line, we preserved jam, and some slept with each others' husbands. There was still fear lurking beneath the surface of ordinary domestic lives.

Anyway, somebody in our group had read about 'the Pill' being distributed to women of means, in America. There was talk that it would soon be available in New Zealand. The end of the messy, undignified birth-control methods we used, of our dependence on our partners to use condoms or to practise the rhythm method, or withdrawal, was in sight. Every drop of sperm counted, as couples discovered too often to their dismay. If this seems unduly intimate, for the majority of women the reproductive period of our lives, how we had our children, or not, is one of our central and most enduring narratives, the stories we tell and retell, whether it be to others or our secret selves.

I encountered the Pill somewhere in the late 1960s, and the term Anovlar 21 strikes a chord. It is almost certainly what was prescribed for me. By then, by one manner or another, including adoption, I had become the mother of two children, and briefly of three. I had also suffered some devastating miscarriages, and further attempts at pregnancy became unthinkable. I asked my doctor about the Pill and it was prescribed. So what do I know about it now? I have learned that it was manufactured in Germany by Schering AG and there were 21 tablets in a blister pack, which came encased in foil, within a box. One was taken every day for three weeks, and then there was a week without them, during which some light bleeding would occur (an added bonus for women with heavy periods was the lighter bleeding). Later contraceptive pill packs offered 28-day packs, with seven-day placebos, so that women would take their pills on a regular basis and not forget to restart them.

The little green pill seemed like a miracle at first. It contained 4 mg norethisterone acetate and 0.05 mg ethinyl oestradiol. Well, that's what I know now, though it wouldn't have occurred to me to examine the details then. I believe it was a pretty heavy dose of hormones. Unfortunately, it didn't agree with me. I felt nauseous all the time, with headaches, blurred vision and painfully swollen breasts. My reproductive life ended with a tubal ligation when I was in my early thirties. Yet for millions of women all over the world, life changed for the better. Women could plan their futures; think about occupations outside the home without fear of unplanned pregnancies, giving point and meaning to studying for professions; space their children in a manageable way; and, perhaps most of all, enjoy sex in a new and less inhibited way.

With an old woman's eyes I'm still slightly taken aback when I read regular columns about how to have the best sex, how often one might hope to have it, how the best orgasm can be achieved, and so on. It's not that I disapprove, it's simply that the focus of sexual activity has moved from childbearing to pleasure and the conversation around it has altered. In the 1970s, when the women's movement changed all our lives, and the Pill offered greater sexual freedom to choose alternative partners, orgasm, rather than children, became the ultimate expression of women's identity.

There was opposition to the Pill's availability, of course, and it was considered unethical to prescribe it — or any form of contraception — to unmarried women, the very people for whom unplanned pregnancies usually had the most devastating effects. Far-right conservatives and fundamental church groups across the globe resisted it strongly. It's interesting to look at the lyrics of songs about birth-control pills: they are almost all in opposition, and penned by extremists. There was one song, however, that was recorded in 1972 by the American country-and-western singer Loretta Lynn. It was called 'The Pill'. Lynn had had four children in her teen years, followed by another two. She hailed the Pill, singing about her 'overused incubator', and the blessing the medication offered it. The song was a huge hit.

Although my own childbearing years were over, I hadn't forgotten the women who still conceived in difficult circumstances. There were many couples for whom contraceptive failure or unprotected sex led to abortion, and there are still many today. Of course there are. Desire doesn't always wait for a chemist's shop to manifest itself on the way to its consummation. I knew that very well. When I left the provincial town where our children's lives began, I was swept up in movements to demand access to abortion. There are heroines in the history of contraception in New Zealand. Ettie Rout, the woman who campaigned fearlessly during World War One for preventive measures to be taken by ANZAC troops against venereal disease, was one of them. Sexually healthy men, of course, led to sexually healthy partners after they returned home. Subsequently, Rout wrote *Safe Marriage*. This contraceptive and prophylactic manual for women was banned in New Zealand in 1923, but published in Britain and Australia. She also wrote *Sex and Exercise* (1925), specifically for women. She was hailed as a heroine by some, but in New Zealand she was widely reviled for her efforts. The age of hypocrisy was alive and well in her home country (technically, she was born in Australia, but her family immigrated to New Zealand when she was very young). Rout's life has been eloquently documented by the writer Jane Tolerton in *Ettie Rout: New Zealand's safer sex pioneer* (2015).

My contemporary heroine is Dr Dame Margaret Sparrow, who has devoted most of her life to women's sexual and reproductive health. A feisty battler throughout her long medical career, she prescribed the Pill for unmarried women long before it was acceptable. She was president of the Abortion Law Reform Association of New Zealand (ALRANZ) for more than 30 years. In the early 1970s, desperate young women would come to her seeking abortions, which she could not legally offer. In Australia, however, abortion had been legalised, and Sparrow devised a plan whereby women requiring abortions could be assisted to go to Australia. It was called SOS, which stood for Sisters Over Seas. Tickets were booked for the women to go to Sydney in the early morning, have an abortion in a safe clinic, and return the same night. It meant funding had to be found and accommodation for country women provided so that they could catch early morning flights.

Our house was one of these 'safe houses' where women came to stay. They were harrowing times. Not all the women who stayed with us were young; there were middle-aged women, too, who already had large families and were experiencing financial hardship. Added to that, to stay in the homes of strangers and travel alone for a medical procedure must have been an unspeakable ordeal. Contrary to some studies which concluded that Māori women did not avail themselves of this service, I know that some did. More than one stayed in our house.

I was in Parliament, as was Margaret Sparrow, when the Contraception, Sterilisation, and Abortion Act was passed in 1977, confirming abortion as a crime and sanctioning it only if two consultants agreed it was necessary for the mother's mental or physical health. A group of us hung out that evening in the office of Marilyn Waring, the young National Member of Parliament who had vigorously campaigned to legalise abortion and tried to persuade the government of which she was a member to support her. I have never forgotten the abuse that was hurled into the room where we sat. A clearly very drunk and red-faced member of the government stood at the door and shouted that we were a bunch of whores. Other swaying men appeared and berated us.

Sparrow has been quoted as saying that it was 'one of the most despairing moments of [her] career'. She was so disappointed, she said, asking how rational beings could come to such a conclusion. My own memory of that night is that the conclusion was reached not by rational human beings, but rather by drunk, belligerent men who saw the proposed bill as a threat to their domination over women.

However, the act that was passed, disagreeable as it was, opened a chink in their armour. There was a way around it, although it demands guile and good performances of mental impairment to negotiate an abortion through legal channels. Many are performed by doctors of conscience, within the act's prescription. Yet, here we are 40 years later, and the act has not changed. People, mostly men, are still arguing about the moral right of the foetus to survive until full-term birth, regardless of the welfare of the woman who bears it.

Let me be clear about what I believe. Pregnancy is the biggest alteration that can be made to a human body, with far-reaching consequences for the woman who has conceived. Yet in order to terminate the pregnancy at the outset she must go through a battery of tests that no other medical procedure involves. I believe New Zealand is out of step with much of the developed world in this respect. Restrictive abortion laws violate women's human rights, not only as enshrined in the Universal Declaration of Human Rights (1948) but also based on agreements made at the UN International Conference on Population and Development in Cairo in 1994, and the Fourth World Conference on Women in Beijing in 1995. High on the agenda at those conferences was the issue of protection for women from unsafe abortion services.

It is ironic that here in New Zealand people may legally have elective surgery to various parts of their body, including cosmetic surgery that alters their appearance or their body shape, and may decline medical interventions to save their life (except in the case of children whose parents may have refused it on religious grounds), yet women and their doctors risk being criminalised if a woman chooses the termination of an unplanned pregnancy brought about by a second party, unless she undergoes the demeaning process of proving unfitness for pregnancy.

What does the future hold for women's reproductive rights

in this country? Will things ever change? I believe that they will. New Zealand has led the world in several areas of women's emancipation, notably the 1893 change to the electoral act that gave all women the right to vote. I do not believe that women have stopped fighting for justice and personal freedom. Everywhere I look, young people are changing in the way they see the world. They make mistakes from time to time, and a tragic few cannot see past the immediate despair of their circumstances, but there are many thousands more who recognise that the way forward is a more forgiving and tolerant society. Younger people are entering Parliament, and more of them are women. The rise of the left with its inclusive mix of young men and women convinces me that the old ideologies of the past are being left behind. The right of women to control their fertility will, I hope, be understood not just as a personal freedom, although that matters too, but also as a measure of social justice and equality, and of improved relationships between the sexes.

HOLLY
WALKER

WHAT WILL I TELL MY DAUGHTERS?

TITLE:	Badge, 'Women can do anything'
PRODUCTION:	Maker unknown, 1970s–1980s
MATERIALS:	Tin, paper, plastic
DIMENSIONS:	44 mm (diameter)
CREDIT:	Gift of Anne Else, 2004
REGISTRATION:	GH014496

1.

I'm hours away from giving birth to my second daughter, leaking amniotic fluid into a giant maternity pad, and marching through a labyrinth. I'm not lost: the labyrinth is a two-dimensional mosaic, set into the grounds of Hutt Hospital. There's one meandering path into the centre and out again, intended for people to walk in quiet contemplation as they await news of a loved one, perhaps grieve a loss, or, in my case, wait for a baby.

Half an hour ago, my midwife Suzanne broke my waters with a blunt instrument resembling a crochet hook. We're hoping this will be enough to get things moving. Even though I'm 15 days past my due date, I'm determined to attempt a vaginal birth with as little intervention as possible. The duty obstetrician thinks I'm crazy, especially because a scan has indicated the baby is unusually large. 'There's a reason you haven't gone into labour on your own yet,' she tells me. 'Your baby is very big and there is a risk she may get stuck.' I politely say I'd still like to try it my way. She looks exasperated but she agrees.

So now I'm stomping around the looping path, willing the baby to move down in my pelvis, trying to prove that obstetrician wrong. Every so often there's another gush of fluid, but I'm still not having contractions. While I stomp, I'm listening to Hillary Rodham Clinton reading her book *What Happened*, a post-match dissection of the 2016 US presidential election. It's a question women (and men) around the world have been asking in increasing horror as we watch Donald Trump's surreal presidency unfold.

I feel fortunate that the baby I'm hours away from delivering, and her big sister, will grow up in New Zealand, the country that, 125 years ago, was the first to recognise women's right to vote. We've already had three women prime ministers, the latest of whom, my contemporary Jacinda Ardern, provides a welcome and hopeful antipodean counterpoint to Trump's presidency. The Labour-led government elected in 2017, with its commitments to paid parental leave, equal pay, addressing sexual and domestic violence, reducing child poverty and combating climate change, leaves me a lot more hopeful about my girls' future than the previous National-led government did. Later, when they hold their mother's life up to the spotlight, my daughters will also see that I was once a Member of Parliament, one of the youngest women ever elected in New Zealand, and dedicated to making change on these same issues. That's something.

When Clinton announced her candidacy for the US presidency in 2015, she said, 'I wish my mother could have been with us longer. [...] I wish she could have seen the America we're going to build together. [...] An America where a father can tell his daughter: yes, you can be anything you want to be.[1] Even president of the United States.'

Conceding to Trump in the early hours of 9 November 2016, she tried to reassure those daughters: 'To all the little girls who are watching this, never doubt that you are valuable and powerful and deserving of every chance and opportunity in the world to pursue and achieve your own dreams.' In the light of what had just happened, this promise struck a hollow note.

Of course, every little girl deserves the chance to pursue her dreams, but they had just watched the most qualified candidate ever for the office of president of the United States lose to a sexist, racist, bungling fool. What hope is there?

I complete the labyrinth just as Clinton completes her chapter on women's sexual and reproductive rights. Still no contractions. Resigned now to a chemical induction, I head up to the maternity ward. I am preparing to hold my new daughter — with all her potential and possibility — for the first time, and I'm thinking about the ways in which my own sense of possibility has shrunk since I gave birth to her sister four years ago.

I grew up believing women can do anything. What will I tell my daughters?

2.

As a child, I wanted for nothing: a safe home, healthy food, warm clothing, books everywhere, a secure attachment to first one and then two loving caregivers, a great education, time spent outdoors, and lots of extracurricular activities. Some of these things were precarious at first — Mum relied on the DPB, the Training Incentive Allowance and council housing when she found herself unexpectedly on her own when I was born — but I count it among my list of privileges that these supports were available and sufficient. My mum, joined later by my step-dad, parented me largely free of traditional gender assumptions. I had ballet and piano lessons, yes, but also played with Meccano and electronics kits and spent holidays tramping and leaping off high branches into rivers. I was a bright kid, given every opportunity, and I thrived. At primary school, I drew the meticulously straight lines under the titles in my exercise books with a *Girls can do anything* ruler. I don't remember how it came into my possession, just what I thought in response: Of course we can. I'd never considered otherwise.

School reports were glowing, my parents were supportive, and I was encouraged to follow my ambitions. These took me to study law at Otago (swiftly traded in for the more enjoyable subjects of English and politics), saw me become editor of the student magazine, got me a job inside Parliament advising the Green MPs, won me a Rhodes Scholarship, and ultimately saw me elected to Parliament in 2011, aged 29. Once there, and happily shacked up with my partner Dave, having a baby simply seemed like the next step. I knew it might be challenging to combine parenting with Parliament, but I didn't see any reason not to try. Our first daughter, Esther, was born in October 2013.

I should have had an inkling that having a baby in Parliament might be more complicated than I expected when my mum, who up until this point had wholeheartedly encouraged my political ambitions, started saying things like 'it's not going to be easy, Holly' and 'if only you didn't have to go back so soon'. She was right, of course, but I didn't want to hear it.

What do we tell our daughters? It seems it's never easy.

It did not go well. There was extreme anxiety. There was rage. There was self-doubt. Most frightening of all, there was self-harm. And in the middle of the chaos there was a baby watching my every move. It was too much. I stepped down ahead of the 2014 election. I had discovered my limits.

3.

My heart is racing and I'm short of breath as I'm ushered into the studio. It's not the first time I've been live on RNZ — I did it many times as an MP — but this time it's different. I'm about to be interviewed by Kim Hill for the *Saturday Morning* programme's 277,000 listeners about the book I have written about my experience, and I know she's going to ask me about the most personal things: my marriage, my mental health.

The book's only review so far, by former ACT MP Deborah Coddington, has proved controversial. While Coddington thinks the book is worthwhile and praises my candour, she believes I should have known better than to try having a baby in Parliament, wonders why I didn't see the hard times coming, why I didn't let on the extent of my fear to family and colleagues and accept more support. She herself had her children young and started her parliamentary career later, when they were grown. She concludes, 'You actually can have it all. Just not all at the same time.'

'Having it all'. That old chestnut. The evil cousin of 'Women can do anything'; now we must do everything.

My contemporaries are outraged. Green candidate Golriz Ghahraman tweets: 'I can't wait for the twin piece telling young male MPs they can't have it all at the same time, "Wait and raise your kids first guys". Right?' Others contact The Spinoff's books editor, Steve Braunias, and demand he remove the review. Coddington even leaves Twitter temporarily in the aftermath.

I know that Hill will want to get into this and I'm not sure what I will say. She's gentle — she seems concerned to know whether I'm being kinder to myself than I was during the events the book describes — but she also leaves me exposed. The interview turns on that question of whether women can 'have it all', or whether there is in fact a biological imperative that makes it easier for men to work while women stay home and care for babies. I don't know what I think. I want to defend the right of women to be supported to try, but I also know I won't be going anywhere near a place of work with my second baby for as long as I can afford to stay away. 'You haven't figured this stuff out yet, have you?' Hill asks, and she's right. I haven't.

The thing is, while I appreciate the support (I, too, found the review judgmental and condescending), I'm not entirely sure Coddington is wrong, at least about the having it all at the same time part. Yes, there's a deep and unfair double standard, but the way Parliament (and most other workplaces) are currently set up, it's just not true that it's as easy for a woman to become a parent while maintaining a career as it is for a man. This is why we don't see paid parental leave taken up in equal measure by men and women.

The debate will play out again a few months later when Jacinda Ardern, newly elected prime minister, announces she is pregnant and is asked about her plans for childcare, as if it may have a bearing on her ability in the job. Again, I'm torn between sharing the outrage of many, and concern that if we silence questions about how hard it is, we shut down the conversation that might lead to changes that make it easier. Somehow, we have to start talking about this stuff in public without falling into the trap of debating the choices of individual women.

4.

Back inside the hospital I agree to start the drip of synthetic oxytocin that will chemically induce labour. It takes a few hours and increases in dose to kick in, but by mid-afternoon I'm having regular contractions at last. It feels good for my body to finally be doing something productive to bring the birth closer. For two and a half hours I'm able to breathe steadily through the contractions, standing and rocking up onto the balls of my feet with each one. I can even manage a visit from my mum and Esther, who has been collected from day care. But then the contractions start coming one on top of the other with barely a break in between. It's relentless and overwhelming. My mum and Esther clear out, and I begin to bellow.

After a while I start to talk about an epidural, something I swore I wouldn't do. Soon I'm begging. The process is set in motion, but there are various delays. We will need 10 good minutes of monitoring, meaning I'll need to stop moving around so much — no easy feat. Eventually we achieve this, but the doctor who will need to approve me for the epidural is expressing milk for her own baby. After 20 minutes more she arrives, signs the paperwork, and sends for the anaesthetist. The anaesthetist is doing another woman's epidural and takes another 15 minutes. All the while I'm growing increasingly desperate. How much longer?

At last the anaesthetist arrives, and starts giving me the

safety briefing that she must impart to obtain my informed consent. I give it. Then she asks me to sit on the edge of the bed with my feet on a chair, and to curve my spine forward. I try, but it's impossible, unbearable. Another contraction starts and I leap involuntarily to my feet. I'm now standing in the middle of the delivery room on a chair, naked from the waist down. I can tell everyone is worried I'm about to fall, but I can't move, and I'm laughing, too, because this is ridiculous. We decide I will wait out one more contraction, then try again for the epidural. But with that next contraction comes a new sensation, one familiar from my first birth. 'I'm pushing,' I bellow, and within a few seconds I'm on the bed on my hands and knees, the midwife and anaesthetist scrambling to assemble the birth kit.

'You don't need me anymore,' sings the anaesthetist, 'congratulations in advance!' and she's gone. It's just me, Dave and Suzanne. I lean on the back of the hospital bed, burying my face in the starchy sheet, and push. In just a few minutes, it's over.

I hear a little mewling sound. Suzanne encourages me to reach between my legs and pick up my baby. Her slippery little body is warm and pink, her eyes wide open, head turning from side to side. She does not cry. I turn onto my back and place her wet warmth onto my chest. I'm crying and laughing at the sheer craziness of that birth, and the elation now that this incredible creature is on my chest. With barely an effort she finds my breast, and there we stay for the next hour or so, Dave on the other side of the bed, Suzanne periodically changing the blood-soaked pads beneath me, as we stare in wonder at this girl, who is clearly from the same pool, but somehow still so different from her big sister. It is magical. When she is weighed she is 11 pounds.

I had thought I could not do it, and yet I have done it. I think, if I can do that, I can do anything.

5.

We name her Ngaire, after the Mutton Birds song. When she is five weeks old, there is some hope! Parliament's new Speaker, Trevor Mallard, holds the daughter of Labour MP Willow-Jean Prime on his lap during debate on the government bill extending paid parental leave to 26 weeks by 2020. It's a beautiful sight, though I'm sure it's at least partly contrived for the cameras — there's really no earthly reason why he should be holding her at this moment. Behind it, though, sits a genuine commitment to make Parliament more family-friendly. After all those years with a bully-boy reputation, this will be Mallard's legacy. He will review Parliament's standing orders, look for ways they could change to support MPs with babies.

How do I know this commitment runs deeper than just for show? Because he shows up on my doorstep not once but twice, bearing pasta meals for our freezer. They're delicious. He tells John Campbell on RNZ's *Checkpoint* that he was shocked to read in my book what a hard time I had and wants to make sure it's easier for other MPs who are new mums.

It's bittersweet, hearing this, watching the news of babies in the New Zealand Parliament make headlines around the world, at home with my own second baby asleep on my chest. There's pride that my experience was at least in part responsible for some positive change. There's sadness that perhaps if I were having a baby in Parliament now things might be different. But mostly there's overwhelming relief that I'm not; that I'm home with my new baby, that there's no pressure to leave her until I'm ready, and that my only obligation other than to care for her and Esther is to squeeze in the time to write this essay.

6.

Esther asks why I am no longer going to work, but instead staying home to care for Ngaire. 'So, Mum,' she says, trying to make sense of it, 'the dads go to work, and the mums stay home and look after the babies, eh?'

What can I tell her? She is right, both in our individual family circumstance and at the aggregate level. She doesn't remember when I went back to Parliament when she was four months old; doesn't remember being cared for full time by her dad. I hope she doesn't remember, please let her not remember, what that did to my mental health, what she witnessed.

Instead of answering, I deflect back to her, and ask what she wants to be when she grows up. The answer varies, but lately it's been some version of 'a doctor, an artist and a mum'. Today, though, she's dropped the doctor. I ask why. 'Because I will be too busy looking after my baby, Mum.'

Perhaps she's been listening to me more closely than I give her credit for.

I can't fault her: my priorities these days are the same. I don't know whether to celebrate her practical sense, or lament that at four, she's seen enough of the world to reach this

WHAT WILL I TELL MY DAUGHTERS?

conclusion, even if she changes her mind again tomorrow. I can at least rejoice that she's leaving room for creativity. And I can hope that some of the parameters will have changed by the time she's grown.

'You can be and do anything you like when you grow up,' I tell her. 'Even a doctor.'

'I know, Mum,' she says. 'That's why I'm going to be an artist and a mum.'

---

1   Clinton's choice of 'father' here jars every time I read this quote. Why not 'mother', to echo the reference to Clinton's own mother? Or even 'parent'? I suspect the explanation is deeply rooted in the internalised sexism of American society, and was arrived at after carefully testing the responses of likely voters. Girls may be able to do anything, but only if sanctioned by their fathers.

**BEN
SCHRADER**

AT THE FOREFRONT

TITLE:	Badge, 'Women against the Tour'
PRODUCTION:	Maker unknown, 1981
MATERIALS:	Tin, paper, ink, plastic
DIMENSIONS:	44 mm (diameter)
CREDIT:	Gift of Annette Anderson, 2009
REGISTRATION:	GH012534

I'm sure many people wore the 'Women against the Tour' badge, but it's not one that I distinctly recall from the agitated winter of 1981, when the South African rugby team (the Springboks) toured New Zealand and caused bedlam. This is perhaps because the wearing of badges with political or sardonic messages was the street fashion at the time. It was not uncommon for people to wear jackets or coats swathed in badges of all colours and sizes, making it practically impossible to read all the messages before they passed by. I had quite a good collection myself, including a 'Stop the '81 Tour' one. It may be that the monochrome tone of the 'Women against the Tour' button meant it didn't stand out in the kaleidoscope of other badges people wore.

What I do vividly recall was that women and girls were at the forefront of attempts to stop the tour. This included my school. I was in the sixth form (Year 12) at Onslow College, which in those days, if no longer, was Wellington's non-conformist secondary school. The student body was pretty evenly split into anti- and pro-tour tribes. Onslow had no school uniform, but dress defined the two sides. The anti-tour side generally wore ska or punk-rock T-shirts, Doc Martens and army-surplus coats (covered in badges). The pro-tour faction generally sported blue jeans, running shoes and sweatshirts. I was in the first group; my twin, Tom, was in the second.

My tribe met in the school library. There we debated whether the prime minister, Rob (or 'Piggy') Muldoon, would do the right thing and call the tour off, or, if he didn't, how we might help stop it. I can still picture my mate Sarah shooting from her seat and speaking fervently in these debates. Some of us had family or friends who were in anti-tour organisations like HART (Halt All Racist Tours), and we heard about some of the ideas being discussed within these groups to thwart the tour. It was exciting to get this inside information and feel we were part of a wider collective. As far as identity politics went, we defined ourselves less by our gender and more by our age. We were 'School Students Against the Tour', although we didn't have a badge.

There were numerous reasons why we opposed the tour. The girls especially disliked rugby's macho culture and the chauvinism that went with it. This was also true for me. I didn't grow up in a rugby-loving household. My parents saw rugby as a brutal game and banned my brothers and me from playing it. We played soccer instead. I soon learned at primary school that soccer was a less masculine pursuit than rugby and those who played it were sissies.

This didn't bother me unduly. My friend David once told me that he didn't like playing rugby because he often got hurt, but his dad told him it would make him a man and so he had to grin and bear it. As I saw it, the odd kick to the shin on the soccer pitch was preferable to a punch to the head on the rugby field. Yet as I grew from a boy into an adolescent it was impossible to escape the widespread belief that it was rugby that made the New Zealand boy a man. For many, opposing the tour was partly a protest at this mentality and at rugby's dominance in New Zealand's social and cultural life.

The main reason for opposing the tour, however, was that it was immoral to welcome a team from apartheid South

Africa. The idea that people's civil rights and freedoms could be determined by their skin colour was anathema to most New Zealanders. I'm sure even most pro-tour people thought this. The difference was that pro-tour supporters thought that sport and apartheid were somehow distinct; their favourite line was that sport shouldn't be mixed with politics. This cutely ignored the reality that the Springboks represented the racist South African regime wherever they went.

I first became aware of this issue in my third-form (Year 9) social studies class. In one lesson our teacher divided us into groups and gave each a topic to debate. Our group got 'Politics and sport don't mix'. My classmate Simon and I decided to take the affirmative; sport should be above politics, we thought. I remember going home and telling my mother. She agreed it was a good proposition to debate, but pointed out that my father took the negative. This surprised me. 'Why?' I asked. 'Because of apartheid,' she replied.

I knew something about this. During the 1970s our family had supported the union boycott of South African goods into New Zealand to protest the apartheid regime. I'd once asked my father what this involved. Things like wine and tinned guavas, he replied. My parents didn't drink much wine, and guavas were too exotic for our family, so the boycott wasn't a huge sacrifice on our part; but the symbolism counted. If I was aware of apartheid I had not made the link between it and the Springboks. This wasn't entirely my fault. My father was a Presbyterian minister and held leftist political views, but he was not one to share them around the dinner table, saving them up instead for the pulpit. I was in Sunday school/bible class so didn't often get to hear them. Rather than weighty discussions on politics and current events, our dinnertime conversation consisted of family and parish minutiae. It's therefore not totally surprising that I made the wrong call on the debate.

Still, I was determined to make a fist of it. Simon and I decided we needed more ammunition, so we made an appointment with the South African embassy. We were welcomed by a charming and smartly attired official, who led us into an office with a large South African wall map. He proceeded to tell us that apartheid was misunderstood in the West; that his government's controversial policy of creating 10 Bantustans or black homelands was welcomed by the blacks as well as whites (he pointed out the Bantustans on the map), and that politics shouldn't prevent the Springboks from touring New Zealand because it brought two great rugby-loving countries together. We left knowing we'd been spun a line and feeling rather foolish. I now see the visit as an important moment in raising my political consciousness. I don't recall how the debate went, but I hope we lost.

By 1981, I was certain of my politics and that the forthcoming tour was wrong. When Muldoon refused to call it off I knew I had to join the campaign to stop it. The Springboks arrived in Auckland on 19 July — Tom's and my seventeenth birthday — and then went on to the first game venue at Gisborne. I remember asking Tom why he supported the tour. He replied that he liked rugby and believed that sport and politics shouldn't mix. I considered him misguided, to say the least, but I accepted his view was genuine. (I later realised that it must have taken a lot of courage for him to take this position in an otherwise anti-tour family.) After that perfunctory exchange, we didn't discuss the tour further, tacitly deciding to let sleeping dogs lie. He and I shared an L-shaped bedroom. Sometime before, we had strung up a curtain down its middle to provide some privacy. It wasn't always pulled across the space, but during the tour it was fully drawn. I thought of it as our 'iron curtain'.

At school, following the Gisborne match, Sarah and my other mates excitably discussed how protestors had littered the field with glass and scuffled with pro-tour supporters. The next match was in Hamilton and we boldly talked about going up there to join other protestors, but nothing came of it. We were all elated when protestors stormed the Hamilton ground and forced the game's cancellation; it seemed possible that the tour might now be called off on public safety grounds.

Our optimism suffered a blow a few days later following the so-called Battle of Molesworth Street in Wellington. This occurred in the early evening of 29 July, when anti-tour protestors marching towards Parliament were blocked on Molesworth Street by the police. As the protestors surged forward, the police pulled out their short batons and began beating them, leaving many bloodied, bruised and shocked. (A newspaper photo of 16-year-old Karen Brough's bleeding face became the sobering emblem of the episode.) My sister Kay was on the demonstration and the first I heard of it was when she came flying through our back door into the kitchen. Through tears she told us what had happened. We listened in horror, disbelief and dismay. It was the first time in our experience that we had known the police to act this way. We thought it was a deliberate signal from Muldoon that he'd use the full force of the state to ensure the tour proceeded. What a prick.

The Battle of Molesworth Street upped the ante. Anti-tour protestors started wearing helmets and other gear to better protect themselves — badges weren't going to cut it. The police began using their new 'anti-riot' units, the infamous Red and Blue squads, and gave them (more effectual) long batons. The first rugby test was played in Christchurch on 16 August. Despite a concerted effort by protestors to stop the game, it went ahead and the All Blacks won.

The next test was to be held in Wellington on 29 August. Again, my tribe met in the school library, where we discussed joining anti-tour activities. The day began with protestors trying to block city entrances — I joined a sit-down picket at the Aotea Quay motorway exit before police moved us on — after which a huge crowd assembled at Courtenay Place for a march on Athletic Park. Organisers divided us into separate contingents, each defined by a different colour; I was in the pink section. These would approach the park from different directions to disperse the police. We all set off up Kent Terrace and around the Basin Reserve. On the Adelaide Road corner was the Caledonian Hotel, a nondescript 1960s-era building with a first-floor balcony. It was packed with rugby supporters, male and female, downing pints before the game. As we passed, they hurled abuse at us; 'fucking poofters' being the main slur. Some took to biffing beer glasses and even jugs. I'm not sure if any hit us, but glass littered the street. We increased our chanting — 'One, two, three, four, we don't want your racist tour' — enraging the balcony boozers further. I remember looking up and seeing faces twisted with hatred.

We marched past the hospital and our group headed towards Newtown Park. There we all rushed over a hill, coming out on the southern end of Athletic Park. We hadn't been told but I think the strategy was to get into the park from this side and disrupt the game. In the scramble over the hill I'd become separated from the friends I'd been with, but now talked with two women beside me about where we might be going and what we might do. We were rather subdued and nervous. We proceeded to Rintoul Street and looked down on the Luxford Street intersection. We could see another group of protestors coming down the other side — the brown section. Between us was the Red Squad. We were told that the police had agreed the two groups could join and proceed along Luxford Street to Adelaide Road. We moved forward, but, just before the expected convergence, the Red Squad attacked.

I was about 20 metres from the front and heard shouts of surprise and screams as batons connected with heads and limbs with a dull thud. Over this was the Red Squad chant of 'Move, move, move'. Our group surged forward and then back before disintegrating as people tried to escape the assault. I found myself sheltering with others under a shop veranda. Some had been hit and were nursing wounds; some were incensed and shouting abuse at the police, and others were distraught and sobbing. I felt bewildered. I'm not sure how long the attack lasted — maybe two or three minutes — but eventually the police withdrew. I'm still mystified by the attack because afterwards the two protest groups were permitted to join as planned. I can only suppose that some unknown Red Squad hothead spontaneously decided to let us have it. It became protestor folklore that police covered their name badges during skirmishes to avoid being identified.

By now the test was over. News went through the crowd that some protestors had managed to get to the park's southern fence and had begun to dismantle it but had got little further. The only good thing was that the All Blacks had lost. We began returning to town along Adelaide Road, passing Athletic Park just as the spectators were exiting. We were separated from them by a line of police, which was just as well because their mood was hostile, some letting rip as to what they'd like to do to us. I spotted my father and brother Paul among the protestors and we all went home together. We arrived wrung out, physically and emotionally.

The final test was in Auckland on 12 September. Again, police and protestors violently played cat and mouse around the streets of Eden Park while spectators filled the stands. I watched the test on the TV, less for the rugby and more for the skyward antics. Marx Jones and Grant Cole had hired a Cessna plane and were buzzing the park, dropping flares and flour bombs on the field to try to stop the game. I cheered them on. One struck All Black Gary Knight. Nonetheless, play continued and in its dying moments Alan Hewson kicked a winning penalty for the All Blacks. I was quietly pleased: a Springbok series win would have given succour to the apartheid regime. Soon after, the South Africans left, and New Zealanders breathed a collective sigh of relief that it was all over.

Many commentators subsequently remarked that, considering the level of violence between protestors, police and tour supporters, it was incredible no one had been killed. This was something to be thankful for, but the tour had still ripped the country apart. It had seemed akin to a civil war, splintering communities, friends and families. Thinking about the tour still stirs up latent emotions within me. I can recall the intense disdain I felt for those who supported it. Perhaps the only positive thing about this was that it later helped me understand how easy it is to dehumanise one's enemies and then take the next step of using violence against them. My antagonism towards supporters endured in the immediate aftermath, but fortunately dissipated in subsequent months.

Certainly, I now don't see rugby players and supporters as bumpkins and boors. The sport doesn't dominate New Zealand in the way it did when I was growing up. Playing rugby is no longer deemed an essential passage to manhood — my sons both played soccer at school and neither was called a sissy for doing so — and due to the efforts of women like Louise Nicholas rugby's misogynist culture appears to be waning. These changes meant I became more open to watching rugby, and if I'm honest I find it a more enthralling game than soccer. If I have any residual resentment over the tour, it's directed at Muldoon. He allowed the tour to proceed to shore up his support in a few provincial (rugby-loving) electorates that were pivotal to success in the forthcoming election. The gamble paid off and his moribund government narrowly returned to power in November. But the cost was unacceptable. Any leader who allows a country to turn on itself for such cynical reasons is no leader at all. In my book this makes Muldoon New Zealand's worst prime minister, and I hope we never have another like him.

As well as my heart, the tour still engages my head. As an historian, I find it remarkable that it does not loom larger in our national consciousness. When we consider the 1980s the images that usually first come to mind, in descending order, are the 1984 snap election, Rogernomics (neoliberalism), the nuclear-free policy, the stock market crash, and then the Springbok tour. But I'd lead with the tour. Arguably no other event in the country's late-twentieth-century history impacted so many people in such personal ways. Not since the traumatic 1913 waterfront strike had New Zealanders been so deeply divided. You were either pro- or anti-tour; sitting on the fence was a derided option.

This was why former prime minister John Key's 2008 claim that he couldn't remember his position on the tour was greeted with widespread incredulity. We might see Key's forgetfulness as symptomatic of a national 'repressed memory' over the tour that continues to the present. Fighting each other in streets and homes over a mere game of sport is hardly edifying and certainly not how we like to collectively see ourselves. No wonder we'd prefer to forget it.

Yet I hope that the tour will be subject to further enquiry. We know it was important in redirecting the national gaze from racism experienced by indigenous peoples overseas to that experienced by Māori. Women leaders like Donna Awatere and Ripeka Evans (part of the Patu Squad formed to disrupt the tour) became instrumental in showing Pākehā that New Zealand's race relations were nothing to crow about. This led to growing recognition that, for them to improve, long-standing Māori grievances had to be addressed. We also know that the moral imperative (fighting racism) underpinning the anti-tour groups found new expression in the peace movement and resulted in New Zealand's nuclear-free policy.

What we know less about are the short- and long-term impacts of the tour on gender and other social relations within families and communities. For instance, some parishioners left my father's church in protest at his position and never came back. I avoided some pro-tour school friends during the tour and only superficially reconnected with them afterwards. Then there was Tom. We gradually rebuilt warm relations — the iron curtain lifted — but we've never since spoken about the tour. I wonder if this is true for others who found themselves opposing family and friends during the tour. I would hope most are now reconciled; but do they, too, keep their silence about the extreme winter of 1981? Is it time to talk?

When I look at this black-and-white badge now, I recall the women the badge represented. I see my schoolmate Sarah, vigorously discussing ideas and tactics in the library, dressed in her punk T-shirt and overcoat. I see Kay's distressed face following the Battle of Molesworth Street. I also see a montage of the women who were fleetingly beside me on protests; their hats and scarves tightly secured against the bitterness. And then I think about the women not represented by the badge. These include the schoolgirls who went with the pro-tour tribe and the sneering women standing beside their menfolk on the hotel balcony. The more I see and remember these women, the more I want to hear their tour stories and those of others — stories that would provide us with a deeper and more critical understanding of 56 tumultuous days in 1981.

**GOLRIZ
GHAHRAMAN**

LET'S
FIX
THIS

WOMEN WANT EQUAL PAY

OUR JOBS ARE WORTH EQUAL MONEY

"OH! THAT EXPLAINS THE DIFFERENCE IN OUR WAGES"

SUPPORT THE CLERICAL WORKERS EQUAL PAY CLAIM

PUBLISHED BY THE CLERICAL WORKERS UNION

TITLE: Tea towel, 'Women want equal pay'
PRODUCTION: New Zealand Clerical Workers Union, 1985
MATERIALS: Cotton
DIMENSIONS: 463 (width) x 602 (height) mm
CREDIT: Gift of Jan Noonan, 2010
REGISTRATION: GH016924

What cannot be expressed via tea-towel art is likely not worth contemplating. In fact, the Clerical Workers Union tea towel makes me wish more activism by organised labour was tea-towelled today. The tea towel, as activism art, encapsulates the absurdity of prejudice: no one could argue that genitalia are criteria for labour remuneration. Point well made. But to my twenty-first-century mind it also demonstrates a disarming acceptance that the gender pay gap exists. Anyone who has addressed this issue today will know the first steps lie in proving inequality exists, then that the gap is caused by gender discrimination (rather than, say, women's lack of ambition or skill). In some ways we seem to have regressed in the face of a rising apathy that comes from achieving formal equality.

Perhaps we have more work to do today, now that society has ticked off the 'women's lib' movement and all doors are assumed formally open. The assumption of equality places even more pressure on women and girls: we attempt to meet impossible standards on all fronts — from career, to home, to our very feminine forms — while being told we are more or less 'post gender'. Nominal equality is even further from the lived experience for women of colour, including migrant, Pasifika and Māori women, who experience an even wider gap in pay and opportunity.

Denying discrimination in the workplace comes at a price greater than just our pay, since devaluing women's labour is at its core dehumanising, doubly so for women of colour, and nowhere is our devalued humanity better represented than in the domestic and sexual abuse experienced by New Zealand women, the incidence of which reflects the pattern of race and discrimination in the pay gap.

So, prejudice is nonsensical, as the tea towel shouts; but it's regrettably clear we have not come as far as we imagined when we outlawed discrimination formally. Current data places the average pay gap for equal work at around 10 per cent. Voices around the campfire (sewing circle?) whisper that if the median income of women were used rather than the mean (in order to eliminate outlying high earners), the gap would be far wider. Horrifyingly, the gap has actually increased in recent years.

In the corporate context, a 2017 study conducted by the Motu institute found that women bringing the same value to their roles as their male counterparts were paid 16 per cent less.[1] The study focused on 'gender productivity' and not simply job title because part of the problem with regard to undervaluing women's work is that women are not promoted to higher-paid positions at equal rates to men with similar experience and expertise. Deciphering a decade of data, researchers compared men's and women's relative productivity or 'value add' to the company with their pay. They discovered, again, that the only factor accounting for the gap was gender discrimination. The reason studies like this are still conducted and grab headlines is that we still need to prove the gap exists, that it is measurable, and that it is caused by prejudice.

Explaining the pay gap should only ever resort to a description of prejudice and that it is unfair — see tea towel, circa decades ago. On the road to the 2017 general election I spoke on a gender pay gap panel for the brilliant organisation

Dress for Success. Our panel comprised women with diverse career backgrounds, from corporate leadership to scientific breakthrough. I brought my own experience: some of it in legal practice (here and at the UN), but mostly in running for office in a still male-dominated political world. It is always liberating to share lived experiences of women and minorities in an environment where they are acknowledged and valued. No one had to fight to prove the gap, though from force of habit we each came armed with proof. The hardest preparatory question we were asked to think about was, how would you explain the gender pay gap to a five-year-old? (If only we had the Clerical Workers Union tea towel hanging in classrooms across the nation.)

But as the initial mental gymnastics settled, I realised it's easy to explain unfairness to children. A five-year-old would only need to know that boys and girls get rewarded differently to call it out immediately. Children understand injustice on a base level and quickly take a stand to correct it. That's the disarming charm of the tea towel. We know gender doesn't justify unfair treatment, so it immediately tells us, let's fix this. But how much harder to prove this to adults.

The Equal Pay Act was passed in 1972, making gender pay discrimination unlawful. The victory of the act came after broad-based gender equity activism, including amazing work by labour organisations. But the presumption that legal protection alone is enough to tackle prejudice was never sound, nor was it espoused by those movements. Just as universal suffrage has never removed the barriers that obstruct political engagement by ethnic minorities or the poor, legislation outlawing discrimination is nothing without continued affirmative action. Today the denial of gender inequality in the workplace, like the denial of prejudice suffered by minorities, seems in part based on the idea that these groups have had their liberation movements, laws were passed, and new 'isms' were adopted to pinpoint their distress, so why aren't they happy?

The gains in formal equality have themselves become obstacles in achieving substantive equality. Lived experiences of women, and even actual data like that of the Motu institute research, are looked at with deep scepticism. In fact, women themselves often deny experiencing prejudice, citing formal bars to discrimination and no doubt finding it hard to identify their experiences as discrimination, given the surface changes in workplace culture suppressing overt sexism. It becomes difficult to believe that men are still systemically favoured at a time when it is legally and culturally difficult to do so out loud.

Society, it seems, has learned to drown out our protests. This is often the result of public 'guilt exhaustion', or because the system of privilege we seek to overturn is fighting back with more effective messaging, which steadily reinforces the popular belief that gender discrimination is all but historic. One danger of the rising apathy is that it feeds the claim, made by those who want to preserve the status quo, that any affirmative-action measures addressing discrimination are in fact seeking 'special treatment' for women or other marginalised groups. I have learned that when inequity in opportunity and treatment is redressed, it feels much like injustice to the group previously benefiting from that inequity. Denial, conscious or unconscious, that discrimination exists has taken us back to questions such as, why should we help women rise in the workplace? And, shouldn't the workplace be a meritocracy? Of course, a meritocracy is exactly what women are asking for. Indeed, we are asking for — and deserve — the resources, roles and status currently held by others. So the feeling of loss and panic that perpetuates the backlash is real. Substantive equality requires actual loss for the Pākehā men of the status quo. That loss feels unfair, so its empirical justification is vehemently denied.

For four years running, I organised the speakers and topics at the New Zealand Criminal Bar Association conference. It's the largest legal professional conference in the country, so I thought we had best turn our minds to equal representation of voices. The first year, I lamented how difficult it was to convince women to be speakers. I was speaking to my friend and then Green Party spokesperson for women, Jan Logie. I told her I could only get four women to six men. Jan told me to relax because on the day 40 per cent would feel like a female majority. It did. In a world where we are not used to hearing female voices in authority, the women speakers seemed to dominate the conference. It brought to mind the famous words of Ruth Bader Ginsburg, US Supreme Court Judge, when she was asked how many women on the Supreme Court bench would be enough; she answered 'nine' (being the full bench).

She said, 'People are shocked. But there'd been nine men, and nobody's ever raised a question about that.'

Her Honour's words resonate in the New Zealand judicial context. I have repeatedly heard my male counterparts groan with every appointment of a female judge. God forbid she carry a race or other minority indicator; these diversity points are the only possible explanation for the appointment, and frankly, the status quo declares, enough is enough.

While minorities and women are still nowhere near proportionally represented on the bench, or for that matter in the senior echelons of corporate law firms or among QCs, the increase in representation feels overwhelming. What these men are really saying is that it should have been them. That a few decades ago, before the bench was the subject of measures to ensure diversity, it *would* have been them — merit or no. Instead of celebrating moves to eradicate systemic prejudice against women and minorities, there is serious talk of discrimination against the status quo. There is no pause to consider why, for centuries, judicial merit seemed to lie solely in the minds and hearts of Pākehā men.

Denial of prejudice is denial of the lived experiences of its victims, but, worse, it frees us to victim-blame rather than remedy the harm. While the tea towel accepts that prejudice exists, and clearly calls out the injustice, today much of the analysis about the pay gap focuses on attributes that we women should correct in ourselves by way of remedy. We lack ambition, we take too much time off to have children, we are innately attracted to underskilled work, we are not 'leaning in'. Being told we are equal in opportunity and legal protection, while the experience on the ground fails to accord with that, is damaging to our spirit and dignity, just as it is when race or culture is cited as the root of criminal offending without the context of colonisation or socio-economics.

If we were to challenge the analysis, we would note that professional women are forced to meet impossible standards. We are expected to carry the load of domestic and parenting duties while simultaneously outperforming male counterparts and 'leaning in' to extracurricular work commitments in order to achieve anywhere near the same level of career success. Articles about dressing to go from workwear to evening wear, or make-up that lasts all day, speak volumes about how far we have not come while we celebrate the victories of a handful of female CEOs as evidence of an even playing field.

At the centre of the challenge we face today is the steadfast existence of old gender roles. As a barrister, I was always pleasantly surprised that the men I worked with took very active roles in the lives of their children. They did school pick-ups and drop-offs, coached sports teams, and took parental leave to be home during the early months of their new babies' lives. This was all possible because barristers are self-employed. My friends in corporate law had very different experiences. Mothers were expected to do these things, though male colleagues would grumble about it (maternity leave was just 'another holiday'!), and women were assumed to be less serious about their careers; no doubt they were overlooked for promotions.

Fathers, on the other hand, felt it was unthinkable to favour family life over work obligations on any kind of regular basis. They would likely be pulled aside and told it was unacceptable if they tried, because of course they were expected to be ambitious and more committed to the firm. Neither gender is comfortable or well served by the enforcement of such gender stereotypes. Women suffer career stagnation and unequal pay, while men are forcibly kept out of family life.

On a broader level, gender stereotypes feed pay inequity in a more insidious way, as work traditionally ascribed to and predominantly done by women today earns relatively low pay even when undertaken by men. This is most accentuated in caregiving or child-focused professions. Nursing, caring for children or the elderly, and even teaching, are all expert fields that are far less well paid than, for example, work in finance or engineering. This is another point of cognitive dissonance, allowing some to deny the pay gap exists at all. The message of the tea towel — that there is still a gendered disparity in wages for equal work — is of no assistance while gender stereotypes label 'women's work' as far less valuable than 'men's work'.

This came to a head in the so-called 'carer's case', when Lower Hutt rest-home caregiver Kristine Bartlett, with the support of the Service and Food Workers Union (now E tū), took a test case against her employer, TerraNova, in 2012, arguing that the $14.46 hourly wage she earned was less than the rate men with similar skills would earn. Importantly, the case was predicated on prejudice arising from the fact Kristine worked in a female-dominated profession. Five years later, both the Employment Court and Court of Appeal found in her favour, ruling that female-dominated industries should receive pay equivalent to what would be offered if that industry was male-dominated. This is an historic win, not just in closing the gender pay gap at its front line, but also because it goes some way in acknowledging all the ways in which the pay gap operates outside formal rules about pay equity.

The challenge of proving that gender discrimination exists is doubled where women face intersectional discrimination. For example, once Māori women enter the labour market, they earn less than Māori men, Pākehā women and, in particular, Pākehā men with the same levels of education. Again, occupational pay disparity, with lower wage levels in occupations dominated by minority ethnic groups, is a prominent factor. Māori and Pasifika women work disproportionately in caring, cleaning and cooking occupations in the public health and education sectors. This is work funded by the government, making it a clear government responsibility to address inequity.

But race is itself only one factor. Adding religion, disability, gender identity or sexual orientation compounds the challenge. Of course, as society's belief that gender discrimination has been addressed with formal protection grows, so also does its belief that we are 'post race', that wheelchair access on major buildings is enough to make industry 'inclusive', that 'settling' the Treaty of Waitangi through some finite monetary payout is the only way to redress the generational effects of colonisation for Māori. In fact, marginalised groups need systemic reform to ensure ongoing respect and equality. Denial of discrimination, systemic and situational, is breathtakingly dangerous for affected groups. It allows oppression and violence to continue just as it tells victims that their experiences are invalid or, worse, justly deserved.

We can link the existence of the gender pay gap to the other, even more urgent, violation of women's rights in New Zealand today: the alarming level of sexual and domestic violence committed against women and girls. On one of my final appearances before the Family Violence Court in Manukau the judge asked me to explain to my migrant client that 'here in New Zealand, we don't hit our women'. Well, it turns out we do. In fact, New Zealand women are victims of violence at such overwhelming rates as to necessitate specialised family and sexual violence courts. It cannot be denied that this is now a cultural problem, which must be addressed at a cultural level. The pay gap encapsulates this culture because devaluing women in public life feeds degrading treatment across the board. It both reflects and perpetuates a cycle of objectification.

As young girls we are taught to place disproportionate value in our looks and, in turn, our ability to find male partners, because after all we are far less able to support ourselves financially. Thereby we are maintained as physical objects for the sexual gratification of men — dehumanised and degraded. Conversely, young boys are taught that their substantive skills, their ability to build, to design, to communicate complex thought will be their making. Women are dependent, vulnerable and objectified for the same reasons and with the same result in every realm.

So the Clerical Workers Union tea towel crystallises for me not only the unfairness of the gender pay gap, but also the fact that women today have the difficult task of proving gender discrimination still exists at all, despite achievement of formal equality and decades of persistent activism. Denying discrimination places a heavy burden on any victim community to prove and overcome its victimhood alone. And discrimination penetrates society in more pervasive ways, dehumanising us, and justifying violence and degradation far beyond the workplace.

Noting the challenges that come with assumptions of gender equality, we must look more closely at assumptions that we are also 'post race' or that immigration debates are devoid of religious prejudice; part of this process involves listening to and affirming lived experiences of unfairness. Only then can we confidently bring down systems that are keeping us down; only then can we make real change.

---

[1] Motu Economic and Public Policy Research, 'What Drives the Gender Pay Gap', http://motu.nz/assets/Documents/our-work/population-and-labour/individual-and-group-outcomes/Gender-Wage-Gap-Executive-Summary.pdf.

**MEGAN
WHELAN**

MRS SHEPPARD AND MR SEDDON

THE ADVANTAGES OF BEING A WOMAN ARTIST:

Working without the pressure of success
Not having to be in shows with men
Having an escape from the art world in your 4 free-lance jobs
Knowing your career might pick up after you're eighty
Being reassured that whatever kind of art you make it will be labeled feminine
Not being stuck in a tenured teaching position
Seeing your ideas live on in the work of others
Having the opportunity to choose between career and motherhood
Not having to choke on those big cigars or paint in Italian suits
Having more time to work when your mate dumps you for someone younger
Being included in revised versions of art history
Not having to undergo the embarrassment of being called a genius
Getting your picture in the art magazines wearing a gorilla suit

A PUBLIC SERVICE MESSAGE FROM **GUERRILLA GIRLS** CONSCIENCE OF THE ART WORLD

TITLE:	The Advantages of Being a Woman Artist
PRODUCTION:	Guerrilla Girls, 1988
MATERIALS:	Paper, printing ink
DIMENSIONS:	559 (width) x 432 (height) mm
CREDIT:	Gift of Sarah Farrar, 2015
REGISTRATION:	2015-0029-1

The same week I was asked to write about this object, in this book, a friend gave me the print in tea-towel form. It wasn't something I was familiar with, but it combines two of my favourite things — feminism and sarcasm. Tools I have used throughout my life to explain the world, and my place in it.

It led, of course, to a flurry of research about the Guerrilla Girls and the work they do, and have done since 1985. They wear gorilla masks in public and 'use facts and humour to expose gender and ethnic bias as well as corruption in politics, art, film, and pop culture'.[1] Anonymous, punny, radical feminist activists seemed right up my alley.

But that tea towel kicked off an existential feminist dilemma. I wasn't going to use it for its stated purpose — I'm not an animal. Plus, I avoid drying dishes with every fibre of my being. But how to hang it? Maybe if I were a better woman, I'd know. That seems like the sort of thing a woman should just know — womanly knowledge passed down through generations, like how to get a stain out of linen, and how to cook rice.

Maybe it's the sort of thing my mum knows? Or my grandmothers might have, and, had they lived past my teens, that might have been the sort of thing they'd have shared, along with how to have their astonishing strength, their fashion sense, and how they dealt with difficult men. Perhaps especially that last one.

I wonder if it's the sort of thing Kate Sheppard knew, or Meri Te Tai Mangakāhia? Or did the fight for voting rights for women trump such feminine pursuits? Does the fact that I have a busy, successful career mean that I can forgive myself for not ironing my sheets? (And, let's face it, most of my clothes?) Whatever I do, it will be called feminine anyway — I'll always somehow be a failure as a woman.

Along with my grandmothers, I think a lot about Kate Sheppard, and the way she has influenced my life. The freedoms I owe her, the rights and the responsibilities. I was 15 at the hundredth anniversary of women's suffrage. Then, it seemed unthinkable that women hadn't always been in every way equal. I'll be 40 for the one hundred and twenty-fifth anniversary. It doesn't feel that way anymore.

I have a purple camellia tattooed on my arm — the flower because that's what the suffragists handed out to MPs who supported women's right to vote, the colour because it was one of the three they used. I think Kate Sheppard and her compatriots would probably be incensed at being memorialised so. I doubt they were fans of tattoos.

But I have it partly because, as a country, we are so bad at commemorating the women who shaped our nation. I live in the shadow of the Seddon memorial. No matter from which direction I return to my house, I see a giant memorial to a man who opposed legislation to grant women the right to vote. A man who certainly was great in his own way, but whatever Mrs Sheppard might have thought of my life, Mr Seddon would definitely disapprove.

In the city in which I live — Wellington, the capital city of this country — as I write there is no statue of Kate Sheppard. There is a bust at Parliament, some pedestrian crossing lights, a short street named after her, and a sculpture at the National Library. But no statue.

There is a sculpture representing the Rugby World Cup (which I maintain looks like female genitalia), and a statue that includes a dog (Mr Plimmer, on Plimmer Steps). There's a giant alien-steampunk-tripod thing in the middle of the main hospitality strip. There's a Buzzy Bee statue, a lamp post that's apparently a memorial to something, and a life-size statue of Mahatma Gandhi in pride of place outside the main railway station.

(As an aside, when that statue was unveiled in 2007, the then Wellington Mayor Kerry Prendergast told the *Dominion Post* that 'Gandhi showed the world you can achieve social and political progress through peace and brotherhood. That is a valuable lesson to us all.'[2] Because women — sisterhoods — have never achieved social and political progress, I guess.)

Queen Victoria is represented in Wellington; and you have to admire a woman who was so keen on public memorials to herself.

There is another prominent piece on Lambton Quay, and when I asked people on social media to identify memorials to Kate Sheppard, a lot of people pointed to it. But it isn't of Kate Sheppard — it's called *Woman of Words*, and it's honouring Katherine Mansfield. It was a joint commission by the Wellington City Council, the Katherine Mansfield Society and the Wellington Sculpture Trust.[3] It's very clearly a woman, and, you know, words.

It says something that there are so few women we've

publicly commemorated as a country that people could so easily mix up the spearhead of the fight for suffrage and a writer who was born five years after it was won.

If we count *Woman of Words*, Queen Victoria, and Hine-te-Apārangi, who appears in William Trethewey's *Kupe Group* on the waterfront, that's three statues of women in Wellington. (I'd argue whether *Woman of Words* is a sculpture, but I am trying to be generous.) So, there are almost as many dogs as there are women.

Inspired by the work of British journalist Caroline Criado-Perez, I tried to find out exactly how many statues of women there are around New Zealand.

Ms Criado-Perez surveyed the UK's Public Monuments and Statues database, and found that of 925 statues, only 158 were of women standing alone (the figure for men was 508).[4] She found that if women were included in groups, the number of female statues goes up to 253. Of the 253 statues of women, 71 were of women who actually existed. The vast majority of those were royal women, and Queen Victoria was most of those.

Here in New Zealand, there's no similar national register. The Ministry for Culture and Heritage lists 12 national monuments it cares for, mostly for former prime ministers (Coates, Holyoake, Fraser, Kirk, Massey, Savage, Seddon); wars and disasters (Atatürk, Tangiwai, Pukeahu National War Memorial Park); and explorers (James Cook and Abel Tasman).

Overseas, the Ministry cares for monuments at Chunuk Bair in Turkey, Le Quesnoy and Longueval in France, and others in Belgium, Korea and London.

The lone individual woman on the list is aviator Jean Batten, who gets a memorial in Majorca, where she died. Batten also gets a statue at Auckland Airport, and one at Rotorua Airport.

With the exception of the war memorials, that list is also exclusively Pākehā. I could find only two statues of Māori women: Pania of the Reef in Napier, and Wairaka in Whakatāne.

Speaking to Radio New Zealand in 2017, historian Grant Morris identified 26 statues of famous New Zealanders around the country, including only three women: Mrs Sheppard, Jean Batten and Margaret Cruikshank, the first woman to be registered as a doctor in New Zealand and one of 14 New Zealand doctors who lost their lives during the 1918 influenza pandemic.[5]

Kate Sheppard, of course, is memorialised elsewhere — she's on the $10 note, and there are suffrage memorials in Auckland and Christchurch. There are halls named after her, and her home in Christchurch is a heritage place. And this isn't an exhaustive list. But if anyone deserves a statue in our capital city, surely it's that bloody woman?

Or maybe it's not. Maybe it's Elizabeth Yates, who became the first woman mayor in the British Empire when she was elected mayor of Onehunga in 1893; or Meri Te Tai Mangakāhia, who presented a motion to the Māori Parliament, Te Kotahitanga, requesting women have the right to vote and stand for that Parliament, in 1892.

Maybe it's Te Puea Hērangi, or Janet Frame, or Ettie Rout, or Elizabeth McCombs, or Iriaka Rātana, or Arapera Hineira Kaa Blank or Aunt Daisy. Or Dame Whina Cooper or Yvette Williams or Beatrice Tinsley.

If we can commemorate a racehorse — Phar Lap — then surely Nancy Wake deserves a monument somewhere? Or all those other women who worked 'without the pressure of success'.

Public monuments are an expression of power. Picture Queen Victoria, high above Cambridge and Kent terraces in Wellington, solidly surveying the entrance to the CBD amid a beautiful garden. (And, in fairness, adjacent to a fried chicken place, because being a monarch isn't all it's cracked up to be.) She's resolute, imperious, regal. She reminds us where power lies. (She is, of course, also memorialised in Albert Park in Auckland and Victoria Square in Christchurch.)

The statues in Parliament grounds, of Richard Seddon and John Ballance, show us who is at home there. Even the language Parliament's website uses to describe them is about power: 'For nearly one hundred years the large bronze statue of "King Dick" (Premier Richard John Seddon) has dominated Parliament's grounds, just as Seddon during his time as Premier (1893–1906) bestrode New Zealand politics.'[6]

Public monuments tell us who we are as a country. Seeing ourselves in those monuments is important — and not just for the men who happen to look like King Dick and John Logan Campbell. For a country whose national identity is so rooted in being the first country in the world to grant women's suffrage, why are we so coy about women's successes?

Statues tell us what's important to remember — so are we to believe the achievements of women are not worth remembering? Are Richard Seddon's achievements really so much more noteworthy than Kate Sheppard's? More long-lasting or world-changing? If women wore gorilla suits while they changed the world, might people take notice of that? Does everything we do have to be a stunt?

We may have come a long way from Kate Sheppard's time, but even now, the 2017 Parliament had its most women representatives ever, and at 48 out of 120 it's still a long way from equal representation. Women are still paid less, and, yes, many still get the 'opportunity to choose between career and motherhood'.

Everything the Guerrilla Girls were talking about on this poster in 1988 is still true today. 'The Advantages of Being a Woman Artist' is still totally relevant. 'Feminism is one of the most troubling concepts to the patriarchy,' 'Frida Kahlo', one of the founding members of the Guerrilla Girls (who take the names of famous artists), told me when I spoke to her over Skype in November 2017.

I asked about the sarcasm inherent in so much of the group's work, especially in this particular poster. 'Well, we discovered, first of all, it made us feel great to make fun of the system we thought oppressed us.

'In a way, if the only power you have to strike back is to ridicule, or to humiliate, it's very gratifying. The power of political satire is that it is claiming a certain kind of power against domination.'

In 1878, when Robert Stout's electoral bill included the proposal that women ratepayers be allowed to vote and stand for election to the New Zealand Parliament, it was met with some consternation. 'If women occupied seats in the House, one member (female) would probably be engaged in carrying a little Bill through the House, while another one would be carrying one through the bedroom,' said the member for Taieri, Mr Cutten. 'While women were occupied in the House of Parliament, men would be occupied in their own houses making the beds.'[7]

In 1988, it was much the same for the Guerrilla Girls.

'You wouldn't believe the disbelief about our work. Even people of the most liberal political persuasion were very uncomfortable to have a scrutinising eye turned on their own profession,' said 'Frida Kahlo'.

'The art world always took a pass, because they would say, "Oh, you know, art is above all of these earthly concerns. There is artistic licence. We really can't apply the same criteria of ethical examination to art as we can to other areas."'

And in 2017, when 37-year-old Jacinda Ardern ascended to the leadership of the Labour Party, she was asked almost immediately what her baby plans were, and more than one pundit asked if such a young woman was really up to the job. No word on whether her partner, Clarke Gayford, is occupied making the beds. (Though he will be the 'stay-at-home dad' to the baby, the couple announced in January 2018.)

'Frida Kahlo' says that 30 years after the Guerrilla Girls were founded, the group went back to look at the stats. 'In 1985, the number of women artists showing in museums in New York were, like, zero, zero, one, zero.

'Now it's one, one, two, one. I think some people would say that's not much of a change, and that's the reason why we have to keep going. Sometimes it's two steps forward, one step back.'

The Guerrilla Girls have done more than 100 projects — many are what 'Frida Kahlo' calls bridges from one unforgettable project to another unforgettable project.

'There are many, many steps in between, many things that we did, that are not as outrageously memorable as others. We just didn't give up, and we're constantly doing projects. And now we're even doing projects at the invitation of the institutions because within institutions there are well-intentioned people who want to change things.'

I am not Guerrilla. I have pink hair and, as a fat woman, I take up a lot of space — space men usually like to deny me. I work for the public broadcaster, and speak openly on the radio about having depression. My life is very public.

And yet it feels like a lot of the work I do is behind a gorilla mask. Will anyone notice if this show features more women than men? Will anyone complain? If I say Mary Wollstonecraft's daughter invented science fiction, how many people will email in to complain? How many times am I going to have to say, 'OK, but let's not forget women — and in particular, let's not forget women of colour, LGBT women, and disabled women' in a meeting?

If I make a documentary about the gender pay gap, how many men are going to tweet me to tell me it doesn't exist? (Answer: a lot.) If I'm constantly the harpy in meetings — the one that won't let it go — will that harm my career? Will the men, with their figurative cigars and Italian suits, forgive me for caring that 125 years on from women's suffrage, many women still don't get a fair go? Why should I care if they do?

In 1891, a woman's natural place was thought to be the home, not politics. 'There may be possibly some of our wives who would be politically inclined, and who might be in the other chamber,' opined the Hon. John Thomas Peacock of Canterbury.

'Suppose an honourable gentleman sitting in this Chamber were to retire home as usual at five o'clock pm for dinner, and find dinner prepared, but his wife not there — she might be dining at Bellamy's; he might retire to his couch and wake up in the morning and find his wife not there. Where has she been? There has been a long sitting of the House until daylight. What a pleasing prospect! How would he like this?'[8]

Two things: one, imagine the outcry if politicians in 2018 retired home at five o'clock; and two, imagine a man now complaining that his wife was out working till all hours.

It's a while since I've seen such a complaint, but it's not like women politicians are immune from criticism these days. When RNZ shared a series of interviews with New Zealand's living former prime ministers, I looked at the comments on the stories about the various leaders.

Of hundreds of comments across a dozen Facebook posts, there was one abusive comment for Jim Bolger (two if you count 'He's an idiot'), one for Mike Moore and one for Geoffrey Palmer. There were more than 60 for Dame Jenny Shipley. They ranged from gendered slurs like 'vile hag' to unprintable profanity, and many were quite violent.

'Helen Clark and I could give you the long list of counterpoints,' Mrs Shipley told *The Ninth Floor*. 'How people have described both of us, compared with our peers . . . It tells me more about other people than myself.'[9]

'You think, "How pathetic", really,' Ms Clark said. 'But you know, again, when you've been in government for a long time, things start to accumulate. 'The series of grievances — it comes a point when those will overwhelm other things you do and take you out.'[10]

Helen Clark didn't give up, nor did Jenny Shipley. Kate Sheppard didn't give up. Nor Jean Batten or Margaret Cruikshank, and neither did the other women in these pages.

'We were just angry, and we found a couple of things that worked,' 'Frida Kahlo' told me. 'We kept going after it, listening to what people said, listening to their criticism.

'We just kept at it.'

Perhaps that's what the purple camellia on my arm represents. Not just a memorial to the women themselves, but a reminder to keep on being the harpy. Maybe it would be cool if other women got to see that every day, too.

MEGAN WHELAN

1   www.guerrillagirls.com.

2   'Man of the people in bronze', Stuff.co.nz, accessed 11 November 2017, http://www.stuff.co.nz/national/9994/Man-of-the-people-in-bronze.

3   Virginia King, 'Woman of Words', Wellington Sculpture Trust, accessed 21 November 2017, http://www.sculpture.org.nz/the-sculptures/woman-of-words.

4   Caroline Criado-Perez, *Week Woman* blog, accessed 1 November 2017, https://weekwoman.wordpress.com/2017/04/17/on-women-public-art-or-no-seriously-the-guy-does-not-have-a-point/.

5   'The history of NZ statues', RNZ, 14 September 2017, http://www.radionz.co.nz/national/programmes/afternoons/audio/201858526/the-history-of-nz-statues.

6   'Statues in Parliament grounds', 15 May 2009, New Zealand Parliament/Pāremata Aotearoa, https://www.parliament.nz/en/get-involved/features-pre-2016/document/00NZPHomeNews150520091/statues-in-parliament-grounds.

7   Barbara Brookes, *A History of New Zealand Women*. Wellington: Bridget Williams Books, 2016, p. 118.

8   *New Zealand Parliamentary Debate*, 10 September 1891, vol. 74, p. 468, quoted in Brookes 2016, p. 128.

9   Megan Whelan, 'Gender bias and Facebook comments', RNZ, 4 May 2017, http://www.radionz.co.nz/news/new-thinking/330011/facebook-comments-is-there-a-male-equivalent-of-a-vile-hag.

10 Ibid.

**TINA
MAKERETI**

PAO
PAO
PAO

TITLE: Poi
PRODUCTION: Ngaahina Hohaia, circa 2009
MATERIALS: Wool, calico, cotton
DIMENSIONS: 291 (circumference) x 550 (length) mm
CREDIT: Gift of Teina Davidson, 2012
REGISTRATION: GH017810

An object tells a story, and the story it tells changes person to person, place to place. It's like the proverbial pebble dropped in the pond: ripples move out from it, resonances, arcs of meaning. Depending on where you're standing in the water, the ripples will touch you in a different way.

This object is a poi made from blanket fabric and fine golden embroidery. The image embroidered on the poi is of two hands shackled, open-palmed, one face-on and the other in profile. The hands are finely rendered and detailed; the braided rope of the poi is slightly frayed from use. The hands look strong: articulate, graceful, expressive. The poi reads as a feminine thing, though poi have not always been so. I cannot view this apparently still object without seeing movement and rhythm: the pao-pao-pao of the swinging poi beat, multiple hands and hips and feet moving in unison.

One thing to love about this poi is that it belonged to a young girl who used it in kapa haka. It is art object and artefact, political statement and taonga, but it is first of all a poi and has been used as such. The object is alive with all the ways it has been used in the world, and all the hands that have touched it.

This is the story that the poi tells me. It will tell someone else a different story.

The hands that brought the poi into being were Ngaahina Hohaia's. She made hundreds from secondhand blankets, their loose fibres playing havoc with her sinuses. I remember how compelling those poi were the first time I saw them lined up in formation for *Roimata Toroa* (2006). When art speaks that clearly, it can be difficult to form sentences that replicate the encounter. Each poi held a different symbol or fragment of a sentence, each was as elegant as the poi that is the subject of this essay, and together they spoke of multitudes, generations, collective identity, peace, war, resilience, spirit. All of this was apparent in an instant — myriad stories held in the nexus of those many objects and their relationship with each other, and their maker:

> Hohaia's show features over 500 embroidered woollen poi made from secondhand blankets. The blanket is a metaphor for the land. She says, 'Te Whiti o Rongomai and Tohu Kaakahi stated to the Crown that they were willing to share their "blanket", but that sovereign independence must remain with Maori.' Her poi are based on the Parihaka tradition of poi-manu, the use of poi in ritual recitation of genealogy. 'The poi is the manu, the messenger,' says Hohaia. The images embroidered on the poi are derived from Parihaka oral tradition.[1]

As a single parent at the time of the exhibition, I remember asking if I could buy a single poi and, even though the cost wasn't substantial, I knew I wouldn't have enough to spare. The second problem: How to choose one when each was so exquisite?

In a way, now I have been given one. I don't know if it is what I would have chosen then. I would probably have gone for a poi with something more obviously positive embroidered on it: Taranaki maunga; the raukura-three-feathers-of-peace. But I look at these hands in shackles now and I fail to see anything negative. I see only empowerment, embodiment, triumph. Whatever was meant by this image, the poi requires me to think about power. I, too, am from Parihaka, though unlike Ngaahina I didn't grow up there. I have been there only once, to an artists' hui, when I was a young student. It wasn't a homecoming because I was a stranger there and I didn't have the cultural wherewithal to make any claims or connections. My family left Taranaki in successive waves of migration beginning in the early nineteenth century, and I'm only tentatively finding my way back. It is a long homecoming.

This then, is a story about power.

In my origin stories, a Pākehā man and a Māori woman get married due to a pregnancy. The signs are not good from the beginning, but there is a tumultuous kind of love there, anyone can see that. At some point the violence between the pair escalates to the point where something must happen. The thing that happens is that the Pākehā man takes the children to a place where the Māori woman cannot find them. The youngest child is two. He keeps the children hidden by moving from one place to another. The mother does not see the children again until they are fully grown.

I was the youngest child. I carried with me no memories of the mother, but I was given a handful of stories about her, some factual and some fictional. By the time I was 16, I once again had some contact with my mother, and found that her stories did not match those of my father and that she was not who he said she was. Many of the stories I had carried all my life were evidently false. I began to understand that I had been given a mythology that explained my existence as a motherless Pākehā child with some trace of a redundant culture in my blood, one part of me cleanly sliced away by a narrative that made sense of our anchorless lives. My fair skin was only further evidence of the veracity of my father's stories. I now understand that, had I stayed with my mother, I would have been given a different mythology, but I do not know that it would have been more whole, given that the story is inherently fractured. They were just kids, really, and the world wasn't fit for their union.

In my first year of university I took papers in Māori studies and immediately began to see my origin story as a perfect metaphor for the process of colonisation. Perhaps we can all of us, the colonised, make this metaphor out of our origins, but mine was so clear and immediate it seemed like a gift of understanding. This new interpretation of the stories helped with the anger. My ardent belief in the power of mythology is informed by real life events that have never ceased to seem mythical.

For all that the above tale seems like one of subjugation, on the occasions my mother has said that she was solely the victim in this story, I found it hard to believe her. It is not that I don't believe that unjust things were done to her. They certainly were. It is that I find it difficult to believe that my mother could be a victim of anything. I want to see her as indomitable. Even though I have been in abusive situations, I don't believe I'm a victim of anything either. This may be an unrealistic and obdurate position, but the only reason I write is because I am those things. Naive, also. I refuse our victimhood: nobody can make us; nobody has ever made us.

It is the stories we believe about ourselves that matter. The stories we give light to. But also the stories we refuse. The stories I choose to believe are the ones that make us strong. Especially when it is clear that no single story contains the whole truth.

This story could have shackled my own hands, but I would not have my origins any other way, for the mess of them has given me more creatively than an easy beginning might have. And just as there aren't single victims in this story, I don't want to suggest there is a single perpetrator. If anything, we are sometimes victims of our own actions. Everyone has paid a price.

Let me try to explain it another way. Us mixed-bloods often talk about walking between worlds, existing in the in between spaces as if Māori culture is on one side and Pākehā culture is on the other, but I don't think it actually works that way.

There is no such even-handedness. I am planted, primarily, on Māori earth. I grow out of those goddesses you've heard about: Papatūānuku, Hinenuitepō; goddesses who were grandmothers to my grandmothers. When everything is whakapapa, those women become more than archetypes. I can look at my own flesh and see their DNA, listen to the laughter of my daughters and hear their voices. The real world exists at this level. Any understanding of women's power, for me, is derived from this deep soil. Women run families and nations and always have. Men work alongside them in these tasks because they always have. At the centre, the children. To disregard the unique abilities of any one group in this community would jeopardise survival. Everyone according to their strengths.

Superimposed over this is something that came later. Visualise it like I do, if you like, as transparent: layered over the top of everything, drawing lines over the real like borders on a map between countries that are separate only because some white man drew a line there. In this superimposed world, there are a lot of ownership rules. There are a lot of entrenched ideas about how much things are worth, and how they must be used. Things include people, apparently, especially women and children. Men occupy some higher rung in this strange hierarchy, but even they must subjugate themselves to the requirements of their system. In this world, it helps to have evidence of status: legal documents, ownership papers, money. It pays to play by the rules of these superimposed systems, but they still seem as if they don't quite have the density of the real. It is in this world that it is important to have rights to citizenship, to vote, to make noise about equality, to participate in the many buzzing systems superimposed over everything, for there really are many.

But I understand it thus: we who find our feet planted on Indigenous soil walk upright. We are always grounded in the real Aotearoa underneath the superimposed world, but we must move through those superimposed worlds layered above it. We must operate on all levels at all times. For example, the vote is important to me on one level, very important. All those superimposed worlds have become very important to me. But that is not where my power is derived from. 'Man' given rights mean little when you know you are descended from the goddesses of life and death.

This is not simply rhetoric. On good days, I remember who I am, and I remember that all the superimposed worlds aren't real. On those days, it seems a waste of energy to get agitated about the political and economic systems that screw us over, Indigenous and non-Indigenous alike, women and, yes, men too, for what woman has ever looked at her son and thought: yay, he belongs to the patriarchy so none of this will touch him? On these days it is not so much that I live in denial, though that is certainly part of it; it's that I find peace of mind, my centre. Simply, peace. Something eternal. Something beyond what anyone can reach. We all do this. If you've ever spent an entire day at the beach with your babies making sandcastles and swimming; if you've ever gone bush for a day or six. You know this place.

It is from this place that I create. It is from this place that

I respond to the creative work that others produce. It is from this place that I can look at history, and the stories of our young people, my stories or stories of people like me, people with stories that are harder and more painful than mine, and not be crushed. At times like that I need to be able to look unafraid at our thin superimposed worlds and flip them the bird, look down on them and consider them redundant. In the great scheme of things they are.

But all it takes is a slow blink. And then we are down on the beach tripping over plastic. Avoiding home rivers that are clogged with sludge. Watching people lose their basic human rights in Australia. Finding change for a person with no home at the train station in Wellington. The superimposed worlds soon flip the bird back, harsher and more brutal than I ever could. Yeah, they say, you think we ain't real? Look at what we can do to the world. Sure, I reply, but this is what I got. I don't believe in you; I believe in *this*.

In *Paopao ki Tua ō Rangi* (2008) Ngaahina Hohaia's poi transform into a bird's-eye view of Taranaki maunga, circles of poi spread outward from a central circle within which images of tīpuna, whānau and the land are projected. Images appear and recede, light plays on the poi cloaked in sound, some ancient, some contemporary, the pao-pao-pao a spiral dance of time and whakapapa and whenua. My first encounter with this piece held me in thrall, taking me in and down, or maybe up, to a place beyond the abstract, superimposed world I've described above. I felt an intense state of wellbeing, of connection, of transformation. Somehow, I was part of that experience, as close to the mountain and my ancestors as I had ever been, not separated. Not alienated. In a gallery talk about the work, Ngaahina described her sense that there was no linear time, that all things that existed in the past still exist. This is the same world view that informs my writing.

I am alienated from the place Parihaka. I have whanaunga there but our particular family have not kept the ahi kā — home fires burning. Those shackled hands represent a long history of being pushed out by successive impositions: muskets, invasions, confiscations, farming, racism, family dysfunction, sadness, shame. Pōuri. Whakamā. It is not that such things are unmendable, but what took lifetimes to tear apart may take lifetimes to bring back together.

Last year the Crown apologised to the people of Parihaka for the atrocities perpetuated there in 1881, when 1400 armed troops invaded a peaceful village and destroyed everything. It was the first time the Crown had ever acknowledged and accepted responsibility for the rape of women in an historical grievance. The people of Parihaka celebrated a new feeling of hope and reconciliation. It would be wonderful if an apt quote from Te Whiti or Tohu appeared here, or from the women who responded with such grace and courage to the apology, so forgive me that the words that arrive as I'm writing this are from Malcolm X (1964):

> If you stick a knife in my back nine inches and pull
> it out six inches, there's no progress. If you pull it all
> the way out that's not progress. Progress is healing
> the wound that the blow made. And they haven't even
> pulled the knife out much less heal the wound. They
> won't even admit the knife is there.[2]

The Crown has recognised its knife and pulled it out. The healing can begin.

It's important to end, I think, where we began. A taonga in a museum. Contemporary, twenty-first century. Poi. Gentle, articulate hands, shackled. The wide-open palms: alarm? A cry for justice? An embrace? I have told you the story the poi told me, of power and grace — the wielding of it, the claiming of it, how it works in this particular life. A rather abstract foray into the nature of existence. The way art can connect and transform and bring you back in touch with that which you think you have lost.

The image on this poi doesn't read as negative to me because the act of art-making has imbued it with power. If someone shackles your hands and does their best to eliminate your people, and you are able to turn around and make that beautiful, make it soft and musical, golden and feminine, imbue it with strength, then the violence has been transformed. We take the things that have been done to us and we look at them from different angles until we find a way to enter them and turn them into something else. We put ourselves back into the things that have been done to us so that the power returns to us. The story of a Pākehā man and a Māori woman and their children is the story of colonial imposition on a peaceful people is the story of women's loss and pain is the story of our nation is the story of our liberty. Take the things that have been done to you and listen for the pao-pao-pao of the single poi alongside her sisters. Listen to the story she tells you. It is the story of what came before and what is possible now.

1 City Gallery Wellington, https://citygallery.org.nz/exhibitions/ngaahina-hohaia/.
2 Malcolm X, TV interview, March 1964, https://www.youtube.com/watch?v=VGx81G5taD0.

**CHARLOTTE
MACDONALD**

A
RADICAL
NOTION

TITLE:	Reserve Bank of New Zealand $10 banknote
PRODUCTION:	Reserve Bank of New Zealand, 2015
MATERIALS:	Polymer, ink
DIMENSIONS:	140 (width) x 68 (height) mm
CREDIT:	Gift of the Bank of New Zealand, 2016
REGISTRATION:	GH025251

What is Kate Sheppard carrying as she walks to the polling booth for the first time on a summery Tuesday morning in late November 1893?

In the small bag clasped by her wrist perhaps there rest a few coins, a ten-shilling banknote; a handkerchief; a house key (or was such a thing not necessary?); a small notebook and pencil; a letter or telegram of congratulation (perhaps from her one-time opponent Premier Richard Seddon); her thoughts, her hopes?

In 2018 Kate Sheppard is in our pockets, our purses, our wallets and handbags. Her face is on our $10 banknote; the blue one. Sheppard's head-and-shoulders portrait adorns the note that we slide and crumple in and out of wallets and purses as days demand bus fares, coffees, bread, a child's lunch, entrance to a swimming pool, a parking meter fare. Could she have imagined that 125 years after her first visit to the polling booth, women and men throughout New Zealand would be conducting their day-to-day lives with her often at their side?

Probably not. But we know that Sheppard thought deeply — and urgently — about money women earned, saved and spent. She would not object, I think, to finding herself on a $10 note in our twenty-first-century hands. To be able to vote was a vital political freedom. To be able to buy the daily bread, pay the rent and even think of a new hat was a freedom from a stifling dependence that kept women under the control of others.

The $10 note is a reminder of the long, and continuing, search for women's economic independence and equality in Aotearoa New Zealand.

For Sheppard and her many allies the victory of women's

suffrage in September 1893 was a beginning as much as an end. A beginning to success for campaigners throughout the world seeking rights to a political voice for women. And a beginning to what she, and all others who had worked so hard to win the right to vote, could start to *do* with it. They had a long agenda of laws they wanted to change, social reforms they wanted to happen: repealing the iniquitous Contagious Diseases Act, which made it possible for the police to arrest women who worked as prostitutes and detain them for compulsory examination and treatment for venereal disease while letting the women's clients go entirely free; reforming the divorce law so wives as well as husbands could divorce on the basis of adultery of their spouse rather than wives having to prove cruelty as well as adultery; raising the age of consent to protect 14-year-old girls from the 'seductive' approaches of men; changing the licensing laws to reduce the mayhem of alcohol-fuelled violence.

At the top of this agenda, and predating the campaign for the vote, were the efforts to remove women's economic dependence on men. Gaining an increase in the meagre pay received by domestic servants, seamstresses and factory workers, and improving the often dire conditions in which they worked, was what fellow suffrage campaigner and Dunedin unionist Harriet Morison had been working to achieve. The newly established Labour Department appointed red-haired Grace Neill as the first woman factory inspector a year after the vote was won.

But it was the economic dependence of women in marriage

that was the most pressing issue. Under marriage law in New Zealand, as well as across most of the British Empire at this time, a woman ceased to have a separate legal identity as a wife. Crucially, that meant she was no longer able to own property, to control any earnings she might make, or to hold on to goods or property she might purchase, inherit or be given. As a wife her money and her property were under the control of her husband. So, too, was the guardianship of her children.

As convenor of the economics department of the Canterbury Women's Institute, the body formed in 1894 as suffrage committees became a united and ongoing political organisation, Kate Sheppard led this next stage in making equality a material and financial as well as a political reality.

Earlier agitation in New Zealand by Mary Ann Müller, Mary Ann Colclough, Mary Taylor and others, from the 1850s to 1880s, had eventually led to the Married Women's Property Act (1884). This piece of legislation gave women, once married, some standing in law to enable them to now own money they might have, to spend that money, and to control property as individuals. The 1884 law also made married women who earned money or owned property or business liable to pay taxes (though they still had no say in the government that spent those taxes, as they had no vote). But the 1884 law, welcome though it was, still left most women with little financial say in their day-to-day lives raising children and running homes.

Sheppard and others pressed the question, why couldn't wives be entitled to a share of the household income? As economics convenor she took a proposal to the newly formed

National Council of Women meeting in Bellamy's dining room in Parliament: that 'there should be a law "attaching a certain just share of the husband's earnings or income" for the wife's separate use, "payable if she so desires it, into her own account".'[1]

It was a long time until such a radical idea became part of New Zealand law. Only in 1976 did the Property (Relationships) Act lay down the principle that property within a marriage was presumed to exist on a 50:50 division. Even then, that division would only be made when a marriage came to an end — by death or divorce. Sheppard's radical notion that women might be legally entitled to a share of a breadwinning husband's income is still on the agenda: her face on the $10 banknote is a reminder that the goal of equal financial status *within* relationships (and within society at large) has yet to be achieved. Do we pause to consider this each time we pass a blue bill across the counter?

The Kate Sheppard $10 banknote we carry today is one of five banknotes ($5, $10, $20, $50, $100) issued by the Reserve Bank in 2015. This is the seventh series of New Zealand banknotes, the first appearing in August 1934, six months after the Reserve Bank was established as the nation's central bank. Prior to 1934 banks issued their own notes. Sheppard appeared on a banknote for the first time in 1991, as the sole woman (apart from the sovereign) in the fifth series of Reserve Bank banknotes.

The 1991 series marked a radical shift: a downsizing of the British monarch and upsizing of New Zealand people and events. Unlike Australia, which used the ousting of pounds, shillings and pence for dollars and cents in 1967 to bring its history into the national currency, New Zealand at the same time stuck with the Queen and local birds and plants. From 1967 to 1991, notes in our back pockets or purses were the brown $1 fantail, purple $2 rifleman, orange-red $5 tūī, blue $10 kea, green $20 kererū, and red $100 takahē. The $50 note was a latecomer in 1983 with the nocturnal ruru or morepork on its reverse. The obverse of all these notes carried the face of Queen Elizabeth II. In 1991 the $1 and $2 notes were retired, to be replaced with gold coins.

The 1991 notes signalled a confident modernising of New Zealanders' value in and of themselves; now it was possible to imagine we were a society and a country formed by history rather than — or as well as — nature. Born in 1847 and living until 1934, Kate Sheppard was the most senior of the figures chosen to adorn the 1991 notes. Unusually, Ed Hillary — still very much a living and active person — was chosen for the $5 bill. As the note most in circulation at that time, the orange-red $5 Hillary was the popular choice. Not only were Sir Āpirana Ngata (1874–1950) and Ernest Rutherford (1871–1937), along with Hillary, born later than Sheppard, but their public careers were also very much associated with twentieth-century events. Sheppard's claim to fame alone was clearly situated in the nineteenth century. And her depiction — with well-coiffed hair, calm and dignified expression, genteel lace collar — speaks of a moderate, reasoned, polite, even restrained figure. Sheppard was a highly astute political strategist. Her sharp intellect and skilful pen made her a powerful theorist and shaper of opinion. These skills she used to radical ends and radical thinking. She knew how to disarm her opposition, and she is still doing so!

The 1991 issue of banknotes marks an era when New Zealand was undergoing a profound revolution in its politics, its economic structures, its relations with the world (the sinking of the *Rainbow Warrior*; the suspension of ANZUS; the advent of globalisation with free trade and the bold floating of the New Zealand currency; all that was upturned by the post-1984 revolution). Recognising the Treaty of Waitangi as part of contemporary life provoked the throwing of a wet T-shirt at the Queen on Waitangi Day in 1990, the sesquicentennial year marking 150 years of modern nationhood. But it also had resulted, just a short time earlier, in the full bench of the Court of Appeal ruling that the state was legally required to act in partnership with iwi in the management of land and resources (the 'Lands case' taken by the Māori Council).

The nation's cupboards were being opened onto a surprising variety of new stories, revealing old skeletons and airing fresh views that led to heated words on many a talk show. Expanding, too, who and what counted as our history (the 1984 edition of the Bateman encyclopedia contained more entries about New Zealand sheep than about New Zealand women). In 1991 Kate Sheppard was one of over 400 women to appear in the best-selling *Book of New Zealand Women / Ko Kui Ma Te Kaupapa*.

Arguments about history were part of the shrugging off

of the old shapes of British-derived national habits and the emergence of a new and local sense of New Zealandness standing in its own ground and using its own voice. Like Australia and Canada, New Zealand did not go through a flag-lowering, flag-raising moment of constitutional independence in the postwar era — as did the newly decolonised nations of Africa, the Pacific and many parts of South East Asia in these years. But New Zealanders took crucial steps (sometimes quietly, sometimes boisterously and contentiously) towards an independence of constitution, politics and selfness. Printing our own history on our own banknotes in 1991 was one of those steps.

Across the Tasman the 1990s also saw a more thorough democratisation and 'Aussification' of the money in Australians' purses and pockets. The 1967 figures on the first decimal banknotes suggested the only woman to give birth to the Australian nation[2] was Caroline Chisholm, the nineteenth-century 'emigrant's friend' (on the $5 note). Chisholm was sent packing, replaced in 2001 by Federation founder Sir Henry Parkes and suffrage campaigner Catherine Helen Spence. By that time social reformer and poet Dame Mary Gilmore had partnered Banjo Paterson, the originator of 'Waltzing Matilda', on the $10 note; convict-come-businesswoman Mary Reibey complemented Dr John Flynn, founder of the Flying Doctor Service, on the $20; the first woman parliamentarian, Edith Cowan, was paired with David Unaipon, the first published Aboriginal author, on the $50; while the big stakes of the $100 were saved for opera star Dame Nellie Melba and General Sir

John Monash (soldier, engineer and national hero). It is telling that the highlights package through which we know each others' histories means most New Zealanders and Australians remain deeply unfamiliar with most, if not all, of the figures on our respective currencies.

As for Bank of England notes circulated in the United Kingdom, these have been more explicitly didactic in recent forms, including key texts as well as historical figures on their reverse sides. In September 2017, Jane Austen became the face of the new £10 polymer note, unseating Charles Darwin from the paper version. Alongside her face appears Jane's characteristically ironic observation: 'I declare after all there is no enjoyment like reading' (2017 marked the bicentennial anniversary of her death).

Winston Churchill and the House of Commons feature on the £5 note, economist Adam Smith on the £20 (issued in 2007 on the eve of capitalism's global financial crisis), and industrial revolution figures Matthew Boulton and James Watt on the £50. Artist JMW Turner will shove Adam Smith aside in 2020. The Queen, unsurprisingly, continues on them all, permitted to age gradually as the face of — or in spite of — Britain's rising and falling value. Does she carry her own head on banknotes in her elegant handbags? Only on Sundays, when she takes money for church offerings.

Kate Sheppard, along with her fellow big-noters, got an update on the New Zealand banknotes in 1999. They were now in polymer instead of paper, and with enhanced security features. The latest update (2015) brought brighter-coloured

A RADICAL NOTION

notes, and more features to deter forgers. As well as having her eyes re-shaded, Sheppard lost two of the three camellias that had surrounded her in previous series, and only one of the original two whio survived the redesign (hopefully not a portent of the bird's diminishing numbers on the white-water rivers of our mountain streams). Sheppard herself was reduced, too, with the new note cutting off most of her shoulders and her dress below the cameo brooch on her intricate lace collar.

Sheppard's ongoing, if physically diminished, appearance on the banknote has been an important part of a growing awareness among New Zealanders of her historical status, the leader of the first suffrage movement to be successful in its key goal. Our pride in the significance of the 1893 achievement is on the rise. It is a notable historical moment in the global history of modern democracy.

If this is what Kate is worth in national and historical terms, what might she bring us in monetary value? What can $10 buy today? You might take your pick from the following: two loaves of quality bread (or 10 of the cheapest budget bread); six cans of baked beans; a bit less than five litres of petrol, or about six of milk; roughly 30 minutes of paid childcare. Will Sheppard slip away as cash declines and is replaced by plastic, electronic and touchless transactions? (Probably not: Victoria Cleland, chief cashier at the Bank of England, and New Zealand's Reserve Bank believe cash is on the rise rather than decline.)

What is today's 46-year-old woman (the same age as Sheppard in 1893) carrying in her pocket, backpack, her handbag, her tote eco-bag as she cycles, buses, walks or drives to the polling booth to vote in the general election? A phone; a key; a memento of family or friend; maybe some cash, including a blue $10 note; her hopes for the candidate of her choice; her expectations of what the day will bring. If Sheppard were to speak from the face of that note she might ask her carrier: What is it like to live in your world? Are your chances, your paths, your purse on the same scale as the man who votes alongside you in the polling station? What kind of fairness has the world made for you?

---

1   Cited in Tessa K. Malcolm, 'Sheppard, Katherine Wilson', *Dictionary of New Zealand Biography*, first published in 1993, updated May, 2013. Te Ara — the Encyclopedia of New Zealand, https://teara.govt.nz/en/biographies/2s20/sheppard-katherine-wilson.

2   The phrase borrows from Marilyn Lake's essay, 'Mission Impossible: How men gave birth to the Australian nation — nationalism, gender and other seminal acts', *Gender & History*, vol. 4, no. 3 (September 1992), pp. 305–322.

**GRACE
TAYLOR**

FEMINIST ENOUGH?

TITLE: Pussy hat
PRODUCTION: Erin Kennedy, 2017
MATERIALS: Wool
DIMENSIONS: 245 (width) x 175 (height) x 20 (depth) mm
CREDIT: Gift of Erin Kennedy, 2017
REGISTRATION: GH018161

untitled

P U S S Y

PUSSY
here pussy pussy
come get this pussy

        puss — hey!
        puss — aye?
        puss — hey — oohh — hip hop hooray — hoe
        — *hoe?*
'grab her by the pussy'
        what the fuck?
no . . . I meant a metaphorical pussy!

like pussy as in . . . weak,
like pussy as in . . . I'm the boss,
like pussy as in . . . less than
man,
like pussy as in . . .
        a pussy that can stretch and bring life into this world?
        mutha fucka, my pussy isn't yours to grab

hold up, I don't have a pussy and I give life

        she gives life

GRACE TAYLOR

> *pussy is reclaiming*
> *is empowerment*
> *pussy is middle finger up in the air*
> *is . . .*

let's make hats!
pink hats
pink pussy hats
let's knit pink pussy hats
domesticated fuck yous
like proud and loud knitted protests
let's march
in thousands
in pink pussy hats — domesticated fuck you thousands
and smile when we do it

> *my pussy was grabbed*
> *by uncle*
> *by that guy in the club*
> *by my husband after an argument*
> *was played with and torn*
> *your pussy hat protests trigger my hurt*

my pussy is an aesthetic
is me being who I really am
my pussy is gentle
and sweating my femininity

    pussy is diverse
    is changing
    is undefined

but is MY pussy YOUR protest?

▬

My name is Grace Teuila Evelyn Taylor. I am a cis female (a term that, truthfully, I only just learned in the last year), a woman, a mother, a sister, a daughter of English, Samoan and Japanese descent thriving and living in diaspora within the land I call home, Aotearoa. I also identify as a poet, a youth worker, a single mother, an activist through love, a teaching artist and a mentor. At the core of all of this, I am a creature of observation and expression.

When I think of the one hundred and twenty-fifth anniversary year of women's suffrage in New Zealand, I think of myself in relation to my knowledge of the history of this movement and how it relates to me in the present. I also think about my mother's generation, Samoan women migrating to Aotearoa seeking a better life and more opportunities in the 1970s. Did feminism impact positively on them? If so, at what cost? Was it fair in comparison to other women in their workplace of different cultural backgrounds? Was it really freedom to work a 60-hour week while still being the ever-present 24/7 mother? Was it freedom to receive awkward stares when breastfeeding their fair-skinned mixed-race children in public? This is how I begin to think about feminism first, in relation to the women in my genealogy.

▓▓▓

I will be honest: I had no idea what the heck the pussy hat was.

Naturally I turned to Google. Articles of support and criticism were not hard to find at all, the diversity of opinions was rich, and my 'afakasi (transliteration of half-caste in Samoan) nature' made me jump from agreeing with one perspective to another. The more I read, the more I fell down a rabbit hole of feminist politics. I started to wonder: Can there exist a true balance between accountability and empowerment within feminism?

My Google search led me to the website of the creators of the Pussyhat Project. They say: 'The name Pussyhat was chosen in part as a protest against vulgar comments Donald Trump made about the freedom he felt to grab women's genitals, to de-stigmatize the word "pussy" and transform it into one of empowerment, and to highlight the design of the hat's "pussycat ears".'[1] Yet as I read through their history and purpose and their media releases something made me feel uncomfortable. The creators of the pussy hat had good intentions, but the exclusivity in choosing a pink pussy hat as the symbol of empowerment to elevate women's rights and the commodification of our body parts speaks of exclusivity to me. I know it can be an act of claiming back, but what about those who identify as female not based on the physical? And why does it have to be pink? What is the purpose of assigning a colour to a gender? It feels like quite a step back in history.

The website also notes, 'The Pussyhat is a symbol of support and solidarity for women's rights and political resistance.'[2] I asked my hearty feminist friends, 'What do you think of the Pussyhat Project?' I received mixed responses. I respect each of them and they all raised valid and grounded points. It was confusing, and I just could not get away from the topic of feminism. Am I a feminist? If so, am I feminist enough? What type of feminist am I?

How many types are there? What is our definition of woman? Am I woman enough to be feminist?

Traditional feminist   Intersectional feminist
    Socialist feminist
        Pm and third-wave feminist
    Lesbian feminist
Liberal feminist   Radical feminist
    Ecofeminist   Fourth-wave feminist
Anarcha-feminist   Indigenous feminist
    Consumerist feminist   Choice feminist
        Third-world feminist

and so on
and so on
and so on.

Overwhelming — boxing and defining a supposed form of freedom into one labelled thing and then arguing amongst ourselves about the right type of feminist? Attached to these types of feminist is a checklist of what makes you '[x]-type feminist enough'. The feminist lens seemed to be mirroring the male lens we have grown up with and actively have to unlearn and oppose on a daily basis.

Judging, judging myself, falling into a pit of labels and anti this and pro that and 'are you enough of?' and 'who will I piss off? and 'will I say something wrong?'. . . that isn't empowerment to me.

Is the discourse amongst feminists helpful? The sometimes hating-on between women about what and who is feminist — or even feminist enough?

what kind of feminist are you tho?
I liken to
yeah but, what kind of woman are you tho?
I liken to . . . *WTF?*
the categorising
and defining
and 'are you enough of'
and 'too mouthy of'
I ask myself,

why does this empowerment
feel so close to what we escaped from?

FEMINIST ENOUGH?

> Feminism = fluid = freedom
> to be   exist   evolve
> it twists on the curl of my son's eyelashes
> soaks on the clothes I hang on the washing line
> drinks from the bank account I use to pay my bills
> tickles the laugh of my sisters
> and opens its arms to my brothers

All of this left me with the question, what the heck is a feminist?

I remember the first time someone called me a feminist. It was 2010. I was a new mum and competing in a poetry slam. At that point, much of my poetry was about my identity as a mixed-race woman. However, at this slam I performed a poem called 'Crown of Womanhood', a poem about my experience of becoming a first-time mother. After the slam, one of the competing poets, a male friend, said, 'I like your poetry, you're a dope feminist poet,' to which I replied, 'I'm not a feminist.' I remember getting quite angry with him. First, because he was boxing me in a specific 'type of poet' category, but also because I had an immediate sense of shock at being called a feminist, something I was not trying to be nor identified with intentionally. In my eyes, all I did was share my stories through poetry, my lived experiences and observations of the world around me as a woman. Was that feminist? What did/do I believe in? Equality for all. Was that ... feminist?

Years later, I find myself wondering, why was I so quick to correct him? What was driving my reasons for feeling slightly

offended? Why did *feminist* feel like a dirty word? Shit, was
I that conditioned to a predominantly male lens back then?
Perhaps it was because yet again a man was telling me what I
was, marking my identity for me.

    Perhaps it was my innate feminist defences responding
to that marking? In recent years the combination of female
empowerment, feminism and social media has provided a
useful tool for voice and visibility for many women. But along
with anything related to social media comes the power of a sort
of hyper-projection of self. Many, myself included, have been
focusing on discovering, embracing and expressing our inner
goddess, connecting with our divinity and sacredness. Which
is fierce, ugly and beautiful. But the social-media platform also
creates a strange, slightly contrived sense of displaying your
goddess.

goddess complex

goddess

god-less

gods-rest

less-god

gods-mess?

confess!

less

god

rest

goddess

I have done it too. Sometimes it has been authentic, sometimes it has been romanticised and at other times it has been a form of defence. Over the years I have played with the concept of goddess being a hyper-human-untouchable entity, but now my goddess journey lies amid doing the laundry, cooking a healthy dinner for my family or having a cup of tea with a friend (and not posting to Instagram about it). What I love about embracing your goddess is the focus on embracing your sacredness. That is something that would be good for anyone. To embrace your sacredness is to honour yourself, and if you can honour yourself, you can honour others. This is where my thoughts of feminism feel most comfortable.

Perhaps it evolves based on the state of our world at the time? The more I think about it, read about it, talk to other women about it, the more I believe there is no answer, and I like that. How dynamic and complex we are as women, as humans. And how fluid identity in general is. I like to think that feminism = freedom. Freedom to evolve, to adapt when required, to respond with urgency and love. To kick ass or open our arms when needed. To name and place ourselves *for* ourselves. Perhaps feminism can't be defined collectively but rather is based on the individual.

I invited others to speak about their concept of feminism, and here is what they shared.

'My feminism is intersectional and radical. Intersectional in that I approach the world through a gendered racial and class lens with the understanding that all oppression is interconnected. Radical in that I believe in transformative politics that dismantle, not reform, sexist, capitalist and racist imperial structures. And then to rebuild with equity and social justice at the foundation.' — Hala Nasr

'For me, it is the principle that I own my body, that I have a right to determine what goes into it, what happens to what comes out of it. It is leaning into the discomfort of knowing I have been taught by patriarchal, colonial and neoliberal-capitalist frames that I am not enough, and that most of the time I believe that fallacy. *We Should All Be Feminists* is an amazing book, bcos she ends up with, like, twenty qualifiers before the word 'feminist'. I would say I am a present feminist over a perfect one. I am an embodied, white, cis, queer, bubbly, long-haired, pierced feminist. But Michel Foucault says, "Do not ask me who I am, and do not expect me to remain the same." I like that.' — Jess Holly Bates

'Feminism is an opportunity for men to learn their privileges within our patriarchal society and call themselves out on how unfair the world they live in is and realise this, then influencing them into a new direction where they generate equal opportunities for all types of women — cis, trans and coloured. Feminism is just the right thing to do. Women are more than just our body parts and what society says our role in nature is. Feminism is about giving all women the freedom to live in a world where they can be their truth and their authentic selves, have equal opportunities and be safe. Isn't that what we all want.' — Jaycee

'Feminism in the European sense had a bearing on my upbringing, especially from my Aunty Irene, who really made sure I was aware of the shortcomings of the male-centric world I was brought up in. All the women in my family were survivors despite the classical expectations of their role in society and the situations they all ended up in as solo mums during the '70s, where we all lived together in one house. So it wasn't the feminist movement as such that I was aware of but the incredibly enduring women who brought me up; with no male roles at the centre of our family I just assumed women had to and could do anything, and so did the young males in our family . . . but it was the mana moana that helped me really find my centre, my Sa . . . Moa . . . In the legends I found warrior women, women who slept with gods, women who navigated the Pacific; through the taupou we were present in politics, through our handcraft skills we added to the wealth and mana of the village . . . we were always present . . . age equated to wisdom, not invisibility . . . saggy boobs and stretch marks a reminder of your procreative power, not your sexuality . . . so it is the mana wahine that has truly inspired me to walk tall in this cray cray word we live in.' — Rosanna Raymond

What I learned from each of these incredible humans is that feminism is required to be multiple things at simultaneous times, to shift and change to suit the position it needs to advocate from, the people and systems it needs to pull into account and the people it needs to empower. It depends on both time and space/environment. I believe feminism also needs to acknowledge and advocate for the diversity and multiple layers of varying oppression that exist and can be more intense within certain cultures. Which usually is the result of an outside system enforcing the oppression. An understanding that sits under the umbrella of intersectional feminism.

I don't identify as a feminist. I feel my many roles — as a mother and daughter and poet and community worker and social change participant — require me to not be a specific 'ism' but rather to focus on a motivation of humility. Making any person or thing or movement an 'ism' is to put together a group of people and their ideas in order to manage, understand or oppose them easily. I believe all oppression is related, so to define myself within one 'ism' for me is limiting my responsibility to be a change agent/maker/shaker as a human and global citizen. I believe in being a good human being, to operate from a place of love, hope and possibility and carry out my multiple roles to my fullest.

So my initial question, 'What the heck is a feminist?', has shifted to, 'How can I honour and empower myself as a woman and mother in ways that also empower others?' In my 34 years, I have been loved by men, cared for by men, supported by men. Men have also abandoned me, betrayed me, lied to me, abused me. Did I want to drag them through the dirt, shame them, punch them? Hell yes, I did, but healing taught me not to hate them. Hate generates hate, a cycle of no evolution. I chose to no longer be defined as a woman in relation to the hurt I have experienced from men, a courage only fully found in the last year. My biggest responsibility is to mother my son into a man:

> Son,
> you are a gift to men
> because of you
> i pray for men
> still love men
> hold hope for men,
> for you.

I am grateful for feminists and movements in history, indigenous activists, mothers and women leaders. I honour you and your mahi, and strive daily to live my life how you fought for women to live: *free*. Free thinking, free living, free moving, free speaking, with love, and through all my relationships and my own contributions to this world I pursue to do the same for other women.

---

[1] https://www.pussyhatproject.com/our-story/.
[2] https://www.pussyhatproject.com/.

ABOUT THE CONTRIBUTORS

SUE BRADFORD has a long background in street and community activism, and is a mother of five. Much of her work has been in unemployed workers' and beneficiaries' organisations. From 1999 to 2009 she was a Green MP, championing a record three private member's bills through Parliament in one term, including the 2007 amendment which removed the defence which had allowed parents to legally assault their children. Later she undertook a public policy PhD with Marilyn Waring at AUT, graduating in 2014. She currently works with several community organisations, including Kotare Research and Education for Social Change in Aotearoa.

BARBARA BROOKES is a professor of history at the University of Otago, where she has been researching and teaching women's history since 1983. She is the author of a number of books, including two volumes on New Zealand's women's history co-edited with Charlotte Macdonald and Margaret Tennant. She also co-edits, with Sue Wootton, a blog on medicine and the humanities, at www.corpus.nz. Her most recent monograph, *A History of New Zealand Women* (Bridget Williams Books, 2016) won the illustrated non-fiction category in the 2017 Ockham New Zealand Book Awards.

SANDRA CONEY is a feminist, women's health advocate, writer, environmentalist and local body politician. She was one of the founders of *Broadsheet* feminist magazine and the advocacy group Women's Health Action. In 1987, with Phillida Bunkle, she wrote the *Metro* magazine article 'An Unfortunate Experiment at National Women's' that led to the Cervical Cancer Inquiry and significant reforms in health consumers' rights. She was a columnist at the *Sunday Star-Times* for 16 years and has won the Qantas Senior Feature Writers' Award and the Jubilee Prize for Investigative Journalism. She has written or edited 18 books, most recently *Gone West: Great War memorials of Waitakere and their soldiers*. Since 2001 she has been a councillor and board member in Auckland local government, with particular interest in the environment and parks.

GOLRIZ GHAHRAMAN is an Iranian New Zealander who arrived in Auckland with her parents at the age of nine as an asylum seeker. She has practised law focused on human rights and access to justice in New Zealand. Internationally, she has worked as a lawyer for United Nations tribunals for the former Yugoslavia, Rwanda and Cambodia, building justice processes after mass atrocities. She holds a Master's in International Human Rights Law from the University of Oxford. In 2018 she became the first refugee to enter New Zealand's Parliament as a Green Party list MP.

MORGAN GODFERY, Te Pahipoto (Ngāti Awa), Lalomanu (Samoa), is a writer and trade unionist. He is the editor of *The Interregnum* (Bridget Williams Books, 2016), an election year columnist for The Spinoff and a non-fiction judge for the

2017 Ockham New Zealand Book Awards. He also regularly appears on radio and television as a political commentator, has authored numerous academic chapters and journal articles on politics and law, and sits on the board of the Centre for Legal Issues at the University of Otago Law School.

FIONA KIDMAN has written some 30 works of fiction, memoir, non-fiction and poetry. She has been interested in women's causes, and broader concepts of equality and social justice, all her adult life. Her first novel, *A Breed of Women* (Harper & Row, 1979), was considered groundbreaking in its frankness about New Zealand women's lives. She has been awarded many prizes, including the Katherine Mansfield Menton Fellowship, the Prime Minister's Award for Literary Achievement in Fiction, and the Creative New Zealand Michael King Writer's Fellowship. She is a Dame Commander of the New Zealand Order of Merit (DNZM), holds an OBE for services to literature and has been awarded the Légion d'Honneur by the French government. Her home is in Wellington.

BRONWYN LABRUM is Head of New Zealand and Pacific Cultures at the Museum of New Zealand Te Papa Tongarewa. A former curator and academic, she is the author of *Real Modern: Everyday New Zealand in the 1950s and 1960s* (Te Papa Press, 2015), which was shortlisted in the illustrated non-fiction category of the 2016 Ockham New Zealand Book Awards. She is the author of several other significant works of New Zealand history and has published widely on the history of clothing and fashion, museums, collecting and exhibitions, and designed objects and artefacts.

TINA MAKERETI writes essays, novels and short fiction. Her story 'Black Milk' won the 2016 Commonwealth Writers Short Story Prize for the Pacific Region. Her books include *Where the Rēkohu Bone Sings* (Vintage, 2014) and *Once Upon a Time in Aotearoa* (Huia, 2010), both Ngā Kupu Ora Māori Book Award winners. In 2017 she co-edited a fiction anthology of Māori and Pasifika writers called *Black Marks on the White Page* (Vintage), and completed a new novel, *The Imaginary Lives of James Pōneke* (Vintage, 2018). Tina teaches creative writing at Massey University, Palmerston North.

CHARLOTTE MACDONALD is a professor of history at Victoria University of Wellington Te Whare Wānanga o Te Ūpoko o Te Ika a Māui. Her publications include *A Woman of Good Character* (Allen & Unwin, 1990); *The Book of New Zealand Women / Ko Kui Ma Te Kaupapa* (edited with Merimeri Penfold and Bridget Williams, Bridget Williams Books, 1991); *The Vote, the Pill and the Demon Drink: A history of feminist writing in New Zealand, 1869–1993* (Bridget Williams Books, 1993); and *'My Hand Will Write What My Heart Dictates': The unsettled lives of women in nineteenth-century New Zealand as revealed to sisters, families and friends* (edited with Frances Porter, Bridget Williams Books, 1996). She has been involved in the Women's Studies Association / Pae Akoranga Wāhine and served twice as president of the New Zealand Historical Association.

BEN SCHRADER is a Wellington public historian with expertise in urban and housing history as well as historic preservation. His most recent book is the multi-award-winning *The Big Smoke: New Zealand cities, 1840–1920* (Bridget Williams Books, 2016). He was fortunate to grow up in a whānau of strong women in which sex role stereotypes were discouraged. His parents taught him how to cook, and it was over the dinner table in a dank student flat in 1985 that he got to know and fall for his lively flatmate, Lis Cowey. He and Lis have two sons, Fred and Carlo.

GRACE TEUILA EVELYN TAYLOR is of Samoan, English and Japanese heritage, was born and raised in Auckland, and is a mother, poet, writer and performer. She has two published works with Ala Press (Hawai'i): *Afakasi Speaks* (2013) and *Full Broken Bloom* (2017), and wrote the Auckland Theatre Company-commissioned poetic theatre show *My Own Darling* (2015). She won a Creative New Zealand Arts Pasifika Award in 2014. She has been part of the leadership for the spoken-word poetry movement in Aotearoa, and has worked with young people in youth development and the arts since 2006. In 2017 she was the Visiting International Writer in Residence at the University of Hawai'i at Mānoa.

HOLLY WALKER is a writer and reviewer who lives in Lower Hutt. Her short memoir *The Whole Intimate Mess: Motherhood, politics, and women's writing* was published by Bridget Williams Books in 2017. She is a former Green MP and children's rights advocate and is now working towards a PhD in creative writing at Victoria University's International Institute of Modern Letters while raising two daughters.

MEGAN WHELAN is a broadcaster, editor and journalist for RNZ. She has been a journalist for more than a decade, and has covered everything from earthquakes and elections to the national jousting champs. Her proudest moment was including a Pat Benatar reference in a story about rugby on the RNZ website. She can be found reading nerdy corners of the internet, creating spaces for women, drinking in hipster beer bars, and wondering when she last fed her sourdough starter.

FURTHER READING

Brookes, Barbara. *A History of New Zealand Women.* Wellington: Bridget Williams Books, 2016.

Daley, Caroline, and Melanie Nolan (eds). *Suffrage and Beyond: International feminist perspectives.* Auckland: Auckland University Press, 1994.

Devaliant, Judith. *Kate Sheppard: A biography.* Auckland: Penguin Books, 1992.

Hyman, Prue. *Hopes Dashed? The economics of gender inequality.* Wellington: Bridget Williams Books, 2017.

Labrum, Bronwyn. *Women's History: A short guide to researching and writing women's history.* Wellington: Bridget Williams Books/Historical Branch, Dept of Internal Affairs, 1993.

Lovell-Smith, Margaret. *The Woman Question: Writings by the women who won the vote.* Auckland: New Women's Press, 1992.

Macdonald, Charlotte. *The Vote, the Pill and the Demon Drink: A history of feminist writing in New Zealand, 1869–1993.* Wellington: Bridget Williams Books, 1993.

Page, Dot (ed.). *The Suffragists: Women who worked for the vote. Essays from the Dictionary of New Zealand Biography.* Wellington: Bridget Williams Books, 1993.

Paterson, Lachy, and Angela Wanhalla. *He Reo Wāhine: Māori women's voices from the nineteenth century*. Auckland: Auckland University Press, 2017.

Rei, Tania. *Māori Women and the Vote*. Wellington: Huia, 1993.

Women in New Zealand, Eighth CEDAW Report. Wellington: New Zealand Government, 2016. www.women.govt.nz/documents/cedaw-eighth-periodic-report-government-new-zealand-2016.

ACKNOWLEDGEMENTS

I am very grateful to Nicola Legat, who had the idea for this series during our many conversations about the future direction of Te Papa Press, and entrusted me with the first title. Nicola is a wonderful publisher to work with and has truly come to understand the power and potential of a museum.

My warmest thanks to the contributors, who responded with vision, intelligence, honesty and power and were a joy to work with.

Anna Bowbyes as production editor added this job to her already crowded work schedule — thank you. Matt Turner was a skilled and sensitive editor. Thanks are also due to Jo Bailey and Stefan Messam for the striking cover design.

I would also like to acknowledge the curatorial team at Te Papa, who collected the objects in this book and whose expertise and foresight underpin this project. My thanks are also due to the collection services team for preparing the objects, and the museum's imaging team for the photographs.

First published in New Zealand in 2018 by
Te Papa Press, PO Box 467, Wellington, New Zealand
www.tepapapress.co.nz

Text © Museum of New Zealand Te Papa Tongarewa
Images © Museum of New Zealand Te Papa Tongarewa

This book is copyright. Apart from any fair dealing for the purpose of private study, research, criticism, or review, as permitted under the Copyright Act, no part of this book may be reproduced by any process, stored in a retrieval system, or transmitted in any form, without the prior permission of the Museum of New Zealand Te Papa Tongarewa.

TE PAPA® is the trademark of the Museum of New Zealand Te Papa Tongarewa
Te Papa Press is an imprint of the Museum of New Zealand Te Papa Tongarewa
A catalogue record is available from the National Library of New Zealand

ISBN 978-0-9941460-0-7

Photographs by Michael Hall, Norman Heke, Maarten Holl, Michael O'Neill, Kimberley Stephenson and Kate Whitley
Design by Jo Bailey and Sarah Elworthy
Digital imaging by Jeremy Glyde
Printed in China by Everbest Printing Limited
Cover design by Jo Bailey. Original woodcut by Stefan Messam